Art in Context

Fuseli : The Nightmare

Art in Context

Edited by John Fleming and Hugh Honour

Each volume in this series discusses a famous painting or sculpture as both image and idea in its context – whether stylistic, technical, literary, psychological, religious, social or political. In what circumstances was it conceived and created? What did the artist hope to achieve? What means did he employ, subconscious or conscious? Did he succeed? Or how far did he succeed? His preparatory drawings and sketches often allow us some insight into the creative process and other artists' renderings of the same or similar themes help us to understand his problems and ambitions. Technique and his handling of the medium are fascinating to watch close up. And the work's impact on contemporaries and its later influence on other artists can illuminate its meaning for us today.

By focusing on these outstanding paintings and sculptures our understanding of the artist and the world in which he lived is sharpened. But since all great works of art are unique and every one presents individual problems of understanding and appreciation, the authors of these volumes emphasize whichever aspects seem most relevant. And many great masterpieces, too often and too easily accepted and dismissed because they have become familiar, are shown to contain further and deeper layers of meaning for us.

Art in Context

Johann Heinrich Füssli, *later known as John Henry Fuseli, was born in Zurich on 6 February 1741 and died at Putney, London, on 16 April 1825. His father was a court painter and an art historian, and forced Fuseli to become a clergyman. He was ordained a Zwinglian minister in 1761, but soon abandoned the ministry for literature and, later, painting. He travelled and studied in Berlin, London and Rome before settling permanently in London in 1779. He made his name in 1782 when* The Nightmare *was exhibited at the Royal Academy. He was elected A.R.A. in 1788 and R.A. in 1790. He then began a series of huge paintings (47 in all) illustrating Milton, with which he hoped to achieve immortality. He became Professor at the Royal Academy in 1799 and Keeper in 1804 and held both appointments until his death. He is buried in St Paul's Cathedral, next to Opie and Reynolds.*

The Nightmare *was painted in oil on canvas (101 x 124.5 cm.) in London in 1781. A portrait of a lady, possibly Anna Landolt, is painted on the back of the canvas.* The Nightmare *is now in the Detroit Institute of Arts. Fuseli also painted an upright version which is now in the Goethe Museum, Frankfurt.*

Allen Lane   The Penguin Press

Fuseli: The Nightmare

Nicolas Powell

First published in 1973
Allen Lane The Penguin Press, 74 Grosvenor Street, London W1
ISBN 0 7139 0274 4
Filmset in Monophoto Ehrhardt by Oliver Burridge Filmsetting Ltd, Crawley, England
Colour plate printed photogravure by D. H. Greaves Ltd, Scarborough, England
Printed and bound by W. and J. Mackay and Co. Ltd, Chatham, England

Designed by Gerald Cinamon

For Camilla

One of the most unexplored regions of art are dreams.

Henry Fuseli: *Aphorism* 231

Reference colour plate at end of book

Preface

When just over twenty years ago Sir Karl Parker suggested that I should write on Henry Fuseli, something of that great scholar's method and precision rubbed off on my attitude to the drawings, so that a number of works previously attributed to Fuseli have been given back to William Young Ottley, John Brown and Theodor von Holst, or at least removed from Fuseli's *oeuvre*. I am glad of this opportunity to reconsider this 'bold and daring' artist, by commenting on his best known work. Cunningham said, 'He had splendid dreams, but like those of Eve, they were sometimes disturbed by a demon, and passed away forever before he could embody them.' At least in *The Nightmare*, Fuseli achieved his purpose.

Nobody writing on him now could ignore the great contributions made to Fuseli studies by Eudo Mason and Frederick Antal. Professor Gert Schiff has been working for some years on a *Catalogue raisonné* of all the works of Fuseli. I am most grateful to him for giving me photocopies before publication of his entries for *The Nightmare* and allied works and material from his commentary. Professor H. W. Janson surpassed the normal courtesies with fruitful suggestions and practical assistance, as did the late Mrs M. Dorothy George and Dr Frederick J. Cummings of the Institute which is now the owner of the painting. Hugh Honour's work on the manuscript went far beyond the normal editorial function, for he generously turned over to me the material he had gathered on eighteenth- and nineteenth-century discussions of dreams and nightmares. Both he and John Fleming gave me real and invaluable help, and in addition suggested productive lines of inquiry.

I am indeed grateful to them, as well as to a number of others who include Alan Butterworth, Robert Cecil, President Georg Eisler, Dr Maria-Louise von Franz, Miss Alethea Hayter, Dr

Herbert Hofmann, Dr Heinrich Kreisel, Dr Josef Mayerhofer, Jonathan Mayne, Professor Herwin Schaefer, Professor Jack Spector, Dr V. Thorlacius-Ussing and George Carter and the staff of the British Council Library in Vienna. Even a short study such as the present one is therefore not the work of one hand, but in many ways a collaboration.

Finally my thanks are due to H. M. The Queen for gracious permission to reproduce works, as they are to the other galleries and owners.

Nicolas Powell
Vienna 1972

Historical Table

Fuseli in Venice where a fever turns his hair white; thereafter he is left-handed. Reynolds, *Dr Johnson*. Wright, *Miravan Breaking open the Tombs of his Ancestors*.	Lessing, *Emilia Galotti*.	1772
J.-H. Fragonard: Louveciennes decorations for Mme du Barry.	Herder, *Von deutschen Art und Kunst*. Bürger, *Lenore*.	1773
Fuseli sends *Death of Cardinal Beaufort* from Rome to Royal Academy.	Goethe, *Werther*.	1774
Fuseli visits Naples, Pompeii and Herculaneum.	Lavater, *Physiognomy*.	1775
Goya begins tapestry cartoons.	Klinger, *Sturm und Drang*.	1776
	Gibbon, *Decline and Fall*, vol. I.	
	Sheridan, *School for Scandal*.	1777
Fuseli leaves Rome for Zurich. Piranesi, *Vedute di Pesto*.	Voltaire and Rousseau die.	1778
Fuseli returns to London.	Lessing, *Nathan der Weise*. Gluck, *Iphigènie en Tauride*.	1779
Fuseli exhibits *Ezzelin Bracciaferro* at Royal Academy.		1780
Fuseli, *The Nightmare*	Schiller, *Die Räuber*. Kant, *Critique of Pure Reason*.	1781
Reynolds, *Death of Dido*. Houdon, *Voltaire*.		
Canova begins Clement XIV monument.	Schiller, *Fiesko*. Beethoven publishes first composition.	1783
David, *Oath of the Horatii*.	Beaumarchais, *Le Mariage de Figaro*, first performance.	1784
Gainsborough, *The Morning Walk*.	Mozart, *Figaro*. Cowper, *The Task*.	1785
Ledoux, Barrière de la Villette, Paris.		
T. Jefferson, the State Capitol, Richmond, Virginia.		
Tischbein, *Goethe in the Roman Campagna*.	Burns, *Poems*. Goethe goes to Italy.	1786
	Bernadin de St. Pierre: *Paul et Virginie*.	1787
	Mozart, *Don Giovanni*.	
Fuseli elected A.R.A.; marries Sophia Rawlins. Reynolds, *Lord Heathfield*.		1788
David, *Brutus*. Blake, *Songs of Innocence* and *Book of Thel*.		1789

1. The Background

When Max Eastman visited Sigmund Freud's apartment at Berggasse 19, Vienna, in 1926 he noticed 'hanging beside Rembrandt's *Anatomy Lesson*, without which no doctor's office would be recognizable, a picture of *The Nightmare*, a horrid monster with a . . . laugh or leer squatting upon a sleeping maiden's naked breast'.[1] There can be little doubt that this was one of the many prints after Fuseli's most famous painting [1]. Strangely enough, Freud seems to have made no reference to it in his writings, though he was, of course, deeply interested in pictures which recur in dreams as well as in all types of dream painting. His disciple and biographer, Ernest Jones, used a version of Fuseli's painting as the frontispiece to his book *On the Nightmare* in 1931 but barely alluded to the work itself in his text.[2] His and Freud's silence inevitably excites curiosity.

It can hardly be that the painting proved too enigmatic for the great analyst of the unconscious. Freud may, however, have considered it too remote from his own interpretation of the significance of dreams. The only dream picture of which he wrote in any detail was a strange fairy-tale scene by Moritz von Schwind, *Traum des Gefangenen*, a much less disturbing as well as a much less interesting work artistically than Fuseli's picture [2]. Nevertheless, according to Freud, Schwind's painting 'shows how correctly the artist grasped the way in which dreams arise from the dominant situation. The title is *The Prisoner's Dream*, a dream whose content is bound to be his escape. It is a happy point that he is to escape

1. *The Nightmare*, 1783. Engraving by T. Burke after J. H. Fuseli

2. *Traum des Gefangenen*,
1836. M. von Schwind

through the window, for it is the stimulus of the light pouring in
by the window that is putting an end to the prisoner's sleep. The
gnomes who are clambering up on one another no doubt represent
the succession of positions which he himself would have had to take
as he climbed up to the window.' And it was with some triumph that
Freud detected in the topmost gnome, sawing through the bars of
the window, the features of the prisoner himself.[3] Fuseli's *Nightmare*
is a very different affair. Nor does it lend itself to such straightforward

analysis. For though it may, like the Schwind, represent the outcome of a dominant situation, it can hardly be interpreted as the sleeper's wish-fulfilment. Depicting a horrific yet common experience, it also embodies many ancient legends derived from European folk mythology, interpreted by Fuseli in terms of the eighteenth-century Enlightenment.

Fuseli's masterpiece has frequently been cited as a precocious example of nineteenth-century Romanticism. It has even been called a 'proto-Surrealistic painting'.[4] But investigation reveals that in both form and content, its ties with the past were far stronger than those with the future. It was very much a product of its period. The aim of the present book is to set the painting in the context of its own time and of its author's life and opinions, to show how and in what circumstances it was executed and to suggest how it may have served as a catalyst for future developments in the arts even if it did not itself anticipate them.

It was with this picture, exhibited at the Royal Academy in London in the spring of 1782, that Fuseli made his name as a painter. The first engravings after it were published in the same year and quickly spread its fame all over Europe. On 30 January 1783 Goethe's patron, Duke Carl August of Weimar, noticed one of these prints at the Leipzig fair and wrote: 'I have not seen anything for a long time that has intrigued me so much.'[5] In England the image impressed itself so firmly on the mind of the public that caricaturists were immediately able to make use of it for personal and political satires, and went on using it for decades afterwards [3, 4, 5, 6]. Fuseli painted several variants of his original composition [7] – probably on commission – but, so far as is known, he never again made so direct and daring a foray into the sub-conscious. Indeed most of his subsequent paintings were illustrations of classical authors and of Shakespeare and Milton; and when these required the depiction of dreams he reverted to traditional formulae [8]. Nevertheless, Fuseli became known – and is still

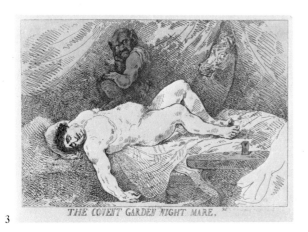

3

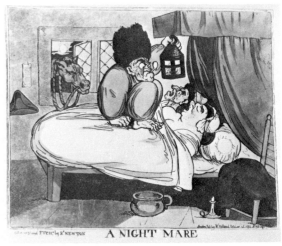

4

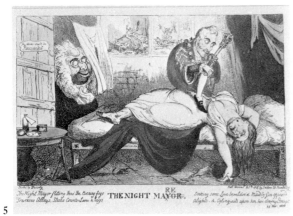

5

6

3. *The Covent Garden Night Mare*, 1784. T. Rowlandson

4. *A Night Mare*, 1794. R. Newton

5. *A Night Mayor*, 1816. Anonymous

6. *The Birmingham Night Mare*, 1832. R. Seymour

7. *The Nightmare*, 1782-91.
J. H. Fuseli

remembered – mainly as the painter of nightmares and 'diableries', to use Coleridge's term.[6] 'His domain was in air and hell, the clouds and the grave', an anonymous writer declared in 1831. 'He had little in common with earth. It was he who made real and visible to us the vague and insubstantial phantoms which haunt like dim dreams the oppressed imagination . . . these things and things like these, were the subjects over which he ruled, and amongst which he revelled, and it must be owned, that often as the attempt has been made, they have as yet owned the sway of no other master.'[7]

8. *The Shepherd's Dream
from 'Paradise Lost'*, c. 1798.
J. H. Fuseli

But it would be easy and misleading to overstress this aspect of Fuseli. His was a complex and ambivalent character. The painter of *The Nightmare* was also the translator of Winckelmann and the stern upholder and teacher of Neo-classical artistic theory. And much of the power of his masterpiece derives precisely from this ambiguity, from its combination of classical and non-classical elements, from its illustration of both rational and irrational beliefs, and from its two layers of meaning – one universally applicable, the other intensely private.

Fuseli was a child of the Enlightenment. Three years older than Herder and eight years older than Goethe, he belonged to a generation that began to revolt against the courtly French-dominated culture of the German-speaking countries at about the turn of the century.[8] Something of a late starter, he was executing his first important works at the very moment when the *Sturm und Drang* movement was in full flood. By a curious coincidence he made his debut at the Royal Academy in London with *The Death of Cardinal Beaufort* [10] in the same year that Goethe published *Werther*, 1774. While Fuseli was painting *The Nightmare*, Schiller was writing *Die Räuber*, the first of his dramas of social and political revolt. This is not to suggest that Fuseli had any personal contact with either Goethe or Schiller[9] – though it is worth remembering that both he and Goethe fell under the spell of Winckelmann (if only for a time) and that they shared a common friend of a very different kind in the physiognomist, J. C. Lavater. The important point is that Fuseli was born in Zurich, then the intellectual capital of Switzerland, and grew up in a cultural world not dissimilar from that of the *Sturm und Drang* – classically and Germanically orientated, anti-French and distinctly bourgeois, in the best sense of the term. Significantly, the only French writer who seems to have influenced Fuseli was Rousseau – the 'citizen of Geneva' and as bitter an opponent of French courtly culture as any German.

Fuseli – or Füssli as his name was originally spelt – came of a family of artists, of bell-founders and goldsmiths, active in Zurich since the fourteenth century. His father, Johann Caspar, was a portrait painter who had worked at various German courts, had become a friend of Winckelmann and Mengs, and had also written and published several learned books: including a history of Swiss painting (1755), an account of the lives and works of the most famous engravers (1758) and biographies of G. P. Rugendas and J. Kupetzki (1758).[10] Fuseli's elder brother, Johann Rudolf, began by assisting their father in both artistic and literary work and later became librarian and keeper of the print collection at the Viennese Academy. He also published a book on engraving.[11] Fuseli's younger brother, Hans Caspar the younger, began as a plant and insect painter and achieved some distinction as an entomologist, publishing what is still a standard work on the insects of Switzerland. Two sisters, Anna and Elizabeth, became painters of flowers and insects. Outside the immediate family circle there was another Johann Rudolf Füssli, a cousin, who published in 1763 the first important German dictionary of artists, the *Allgemeines Künstler-Lexikon*. His son, Hans Heinrich, became Winckelmann's closest disciple.

With this intellectual, cultivated family background it might seem almost inevitable that Fuseli should himself become both artist and art-theorist. And at the age of no more than ten he was copying prints after German masters as well as making imaginative drawings, a few of which survive. In subject matter his earliest drawings range from portraits of glum-faced Swiss humanists and divines to scenes of hunts, battles and murders. But, as Frederick Antal remarked, 'it was only a small step for Fuseli from the macabre to the erotic, as well as to the burlesque and satirical,'[12] and he was soon making copies of fashion plates and Mannerist engravings with figures in voluptuous – sometimes almost obscene – poses. Already in some of these youthful drawings the obsessions which were to haunt him all his life find overt expression, as in a copy he made from Conrad Meyer's *Narrenbuch* illustrating the Aristotle and Phyllis theme. A fashionably dressed woman here sets her elegant foot on the body of an abject, crouching man [9]. Fuseli's artistic education was exclusively graphic: he did not begin to paint in oils until several years later. It was also informal, if not clandestine. For his father thought he had no talent for drawing and decided that he should become a Zwinglian minister.[13] It is said that Fuseli learned to draw with his left hand in order to make sketches surreptitiously while studying or listening to his tutor.[14]

Fuseli was thus given a general education far superior to that of most, if not all, other artists of the time. At the age of about fifteen he was sent to the Collegium Carolinum in Zurich and in 1761 he was ordained a Zwinglian minister. In these years he came into

9. *A Satire of Marriage, c.* 1752–60.
J. H. Fuseli

contact with two very remarkable men, his teacher Johann Jakob Bodmer, and his fellow student Johann Caspar Lavater, who exerted a profound and lasting influence on him. The former was an indifferent poet but a literary theorist of some interest (an upholder of creative imagination against stultifying classical rules and a believer in literature as a product of human emotions rather than of rational thought) and, above all, a translator of outstanding gifts.

He introduced a whole generation of German readers to the works of Greek, English and Middle High German poets. He produced, while Fuseli was studying with him, a modernized version of the medieval *Chriemhildens Rache und Klage* and an edition of the *Minnesang*. From him Fuseli seems to have derived his life-long passion for Homer and Dante and also for English poetry, especially Shakespeare and Milton whom Bodmer had translated in 1732. At this date English writers – notably Locke, Shaftesbury, Newton and Addison – were becoming increasingly well-known and popular in the German-speaking countries, but Bodmer and, after him, Fuseli were probably unusual in their knowledge of and enthusiasm for Shakespeare and Milton. Fuseli remained on terms of close friendship with Bodmer until the latter's death in 1783, the year after *The Nightmare* was exhibited.

Lavater was something of a prig. Even as a child, according to his own account, he formed a special relationship with God, who corrected his school exercises, hid his faults and brought to light his virtuous deeds. Later he was to be described as a 'compound of the intolerant priest and the factitious sentimentalist'.[15] Soon after entering the Zwinglian ministry, with Fuseli, he began to make his name as a preacher of a Pietist type. But he was to secure more lasting fame as the author of the immensely popular *Physiognomische Fragmente* (1775–8), a pseudo-scientific quasi-mystical work intended to prove that the face is the 'magic mirror' of the soul.

Letters reveal that the friendship between Fuseli and Lavater was of a passionate, characteristically *Sturm und Drang*, type. 'Beloved of my soul, how I love you', Fuseli wrote to him when they were separated for a day or so in 1763. 'How I kiss you! My God, my God! When shall I see you again, when shall I lay my hand in your hand, my breast against your breast, against that truest of all hearts, and be in bliss – life such as you desire of me shall at least make me worthy of it . . .' On another occasion he wrote: 'I lay down my pen for a moment to embrace your picture, and kiss it through and through . . .' And when Lavater married, Fuseli introduced himself to the young wife with words which would have astounded, if not alarmed, a bride in any other period: 'I enjoin you to kiss him twice each day *for me*. My soul will often hover about the lips of both – would it were granted to my hand to embrace both of you!'[16] Moderation was never to be one of Fuseli's virtues.

As a result of publishing a pamphlet attacking the son-in-law of a Burgomaster, Fuseli and Lavater found it prudent to leave Zurich for a while in 1763. They went to Berlin, travelling in company with J. G. Sulzer, the Swiss writer on philosophy who had already published his first works and may well have begun his compendious magnum opus, the *Theorie der schönen Künste* (1771) which applied Bodmer's notions about literature to the visual arts and synthesized them with those of Winckelmann and Mengs. This work was to become a key source for German classical aesthetics and, indeed, Fuseli's own artistic theory. But at this date Fuseli still saw himself less as an artist than as a poet, writing under the influence of Bodmer and of Klopstock whom he was soon to meet. In Berlin he began to publish translations from English into German though he also did some graphic work, mainly in assisting Bernard Rode to illustrate Bodmer's Biblical epic *Noachide*.

It was at about this time that Fuseli abandoned the Zwinglian ministry. This is not the place to discuss the problem of his religious beliefs. But it is significant that in Berlin he became intimate with Provost J. J. Spalding, one of a small group of German pastors bent on reconciling Christianity with the Enlightenment and who were known as Neologians.[17] According to Lessing, admittedly a hostile witness, they held that 'all revealed religion is nothing but a reconfirmation of the religion of reason' and though they aimed to make reasonable Christians, only succeeded in producing unreasonable philosophers.[18] This is a grotesquely unfair misrepresentation of Spalding, but perhaps it indicates the position of some of his followers, such as Fuseli.

In Berlin, Fuseli seems to have become still more closely involved with English culture. Spalding and the Neologians were deeply indebted to the ideas of Locke and Shaftesbury: and in Andrew Mitchell, the British Minister to the court of Prussia, Fuseli met a highly cultivated Scotsman who had frequented the literary world of London and knew James Thomson, author of *The Seasons* then so highly admired both in England and on the Continent.[19] At the Minister's house he also met Dr John Armstrong, author of *The Art of Preserving Health* (a somewhat lame didactic poem versifying notions derived mainly from Shaftesbury). Armstrong knew many British writers and, perhaps more significantly for Fuseli, was a close friend of John Wilkes. For Fuseli, like many of his contemporaries on the Continent, was attracted as much by the English political system as by English literature. At this date England was the lodestar of the intellectual middle classes throughout Europe and it is hardly surprising that Fuseli should have wished to go there.

In 1764 he went from Berlin to London with Andrew Mitchell who introduced him to the banker Coutts with whose family he was to be connected for the rest of his life. Next year he published an English translation of Winckelmann's first book under the title *Reflections on the Painting and Sculpture of the Greeks* – a work which had already begun to revolutionize attitudes to antiquity throughout Europe.[20] He soon entered the intellectual world of London and struck up a friendship with Joseph Johnson, the publisher of works by Cowper, Joseph Priestley and, among others, Erasmus Darwin, who was later to take a particular interest in *The Nightmare*. A spell as bear-leader to the young Viscount Chewton enabled him to visit France and enlarge his intellectual horizon still further, for he met Rousseau and in 1767 published anonymously his *Remarks on the Writings and Conduct of J. J. Rousseau* which was flatteringly attributed to Sterne or Smollett.

Fuseli's career up to this moment had been that of a writer. Indeed he had already achieved some success with works written both in his native German and in English. But for reasons which are far from clear he determined in about 1768 to devote himself to the visual arts. He obtained an introduction to Joshua Reynolds who is said to have remarked that if Fuseli were offered ten thousand pounds a year not to draw he should refuse. Reynolds encouraged him to take up oil painting and go to Italy. Financed by the banker Thomas Coutts, who negotiated commissions for him to execute in Rome, he left for Italy early in 1770, travelling by sea with Dr Armstrong.

It would be interesting to know exactly what advice Reynolds gave to Fuseli, for Reynolds was later to exert a great influence on his career in general and, as we shall see, on *The Nightmare* in particular. He probably told him, as he told the young Irish painter, James Barry, at about the same time, to sacrifice all else to the study of Michelangelo, 'the greatest genius that was ever employed in the arts'.[21] Certainly, Fuseli succumbed, no less promptly than did Barry, to the 'terribiltà' of Michelangelo. 'It was a story he loved to repeat', wrote Allan Cunningham, 'how he lay on his back day after day, and week succeeding week, with upturned and wondering eyes, musing on the splendid ceiling of the Sistine Chapel. . . . He sometimes, indeed, added that such a position was necessary for a body fatigued like his with the pleasant gratifications of a luxurious city.' While in the Sistine Chapel he must also have recalled a passage from Winckelmann which he had himself translated: 'Michelangelo is perhaps the only one of whom one could say that he reaches antiquity, but only in strong muscular figures, in bodies from the heroic times, not in tender youths, not in female figures who have become Amazons under his hand.'[22] But for him, Winckelmann's reservations were almost recommendations: he was always to prefer muscular figures to tender youths.

Similarly, among the antiquities, it was the muscular and the colossal that appealed to Fuseli – the enormous, overpowering Horse-Tamers on Monte Cavallo (which he thought were by Phidias) and the even more forceful Farnese Hercules, whose muscles he exaggerated when drawing it. But of course there were

innumerable antique statues to see and admire: the Apollo Belvedere, the Vatican Torso, the Vatican Ariadne and many others.
And already, while still in Rome, these powerful images were
absorbed and fused in his imagination, so that he was able to com-
bine and transpose them in his own compositions, sometimes rather
too obviously so that the incongruity is slightly ludicrous, as in his
Scene from Macbeth of 1774 where Lady Macbeth is all too clearly
an ecstatic Maenad, only with daggers instead of cymbals, and
Macbeth himself the Apollo Belvedere!

For even when in Rome, Fuseli did not take the subject matter
for his compositions solely or even primarily from classical myth
and history. Shakespeare was always in the forefront of his mind,
and he sketched a series of fantastic variations on the Sistine Chapel
ceiling with Shakespearian instead of Biblical scenes and figures.[23]
He made a drawing of Richard III visited by ghosts, of some importance for the development of the nightmare theme; and, for his first
submission to the Royal Academy in London he made a large pen
and wash drawing of *The Death of Cardinal Beaufort* [10]. The
choice of this subject from one of the least familiar of Shakespeare's
plays – *Henry VI* part II – is somewhat puzzling. But it is worth
recalling that only a few years earlier, in 1765, Dr Johnson had
remarked: 'This is one of the scenes which have been applauded
by the criticks [in contrast to others held to be of doubtful author-
ship] and which will continue to be admired when prejudices shall
cease, and bigotry give way to impartial examination. These are
beauties that rise out of nature and truth; the superficial reader
cannot miss then, the profound can image nothing beyond them.'
Nature and truth – the phrase was a rallying call of the anti-rococo
movement, whether in literature or in art, among the *Sturm und
Drang* as well as among such theorists as Winckelmann, Diderot
and Reynolds.

The composition of *The Death of Cardinal Beaufort* is clearly
derived from Poussin's *Death of Germanicus*, then in the Barberini
collection in Rome. (It seems to have also inspired Thomas Banks's

10. *The Death of Cardinal Beaufort*, 1772. J. H. Fuseli

11. *Portrait of Fuseli*, 1778.
James Northcote

marble relief of the same subject, carved in Rome and sent to the Royal Academy at the same time as Fuseli's painting.[24]) Fuseli may also have been indebted to Gavin Hamilton's *Andromache Bewailing the Death of Hector*.[25] But the differences between *The Death of Cardinal Beaufort* and these other works are at least as great as the similarities. There is no trace of stoical calm or classical restraint in Fuseli's drawing. He chose to represent not the peace but the terror of death, to illustrate the lines spoken by Henry in *Henry VI*:

> *Ah, what a sign it is of evil life,*
> *When death's approach is seen so terrible.*

The work is also militantly anti-Catholic, suggesting the futility of the sacraments which are unctuously indicated by a figure on the right. In its fusion of classical and non-classical elements, in its combination of religious and rationalist (anti-superstitious) notions, it already foreshadows *The Nightmare*.

While in Rome, Fuseli moved in a circle of *avant-garde* artists nearly all of whom were northerners. In 1773 Thomas Banks wrote that 'among the students of Painting. Fuseli cuts the greatest figure; last season he had pictures bespoke to the amount of £1,300, good encouragement for a student, yet nothing more than, from his great abilities, he is justly entitled to.' Other British artists in Rome at the time included Gavin Hamilton, John Brown (whose drawings are so similar to Fuseli's), James Northcote, who painted his portrait [11], George Romney and Alexander Runciman of whom Fuseli said, 'he is the best of us here'.[26] Fuseli also knew the Swedish sculptor Tobias Sergel, whom he drew in his studio, and the Danish painter Nicolai Abildgaard, who was later to paint a variant of *The Nightmare* [48]. He also met the young Jacques-Louis David who arrived at the French Academy in 1775.

Fuseli left Rome in October 1778 and returned for the last time to Zurich. Here he painted in 1780 *The Oath on the Rüttli* which commemorates the origins of Swiss liberty and is perhaps his only

12. *Self-Portrait conversing with Johann Jakob Bodmer*, 1778. J. H. Fuseli

13 *(right)*. *Ezzelin Bracciaferro*, 1779. J. H. Fuseli

explicitly political picture. He also began the large *Self-portrait conversing with Johann Jakob Bodmer* [12], master and pupil sitting on either side of a glowering bust of Homer.

While in Zurich he carried on some kind of flirtation with two sisters, one of whom was already married. But he fell deeply in love with a certain Anna Landolt, who did not reciprocate his passion

and the affair was to leave a wound which did not heal for many years, as we shall see.

By the spring of 1779 he was back in London. Next year he exhibited another scene of violence at the Royal Academy, a painting entitled: *Ezzelin Bracciaferro Musing over Meduna, slain by him for disloyalty during his Absence* [13]. It shows a man seated by the prostrate body of a woman, both dressed in the curious costumes, part medieval and part classical, favoured by illustrators of Tasso and Ariosto. The subject was, however, original. 'I have been looking in vain, Mr Fuseli, for some months, in the poets and historians of Italy for the subject of your picture of Ezzelin: pray where is it to be found?' Byron asked him some years later. 'Only in my brain, my Lord, for I invented it,' Fuseli replied.[27]

In 1781 Fuseli began to paint his *Nightmare*, another product of his own brain – and perhaps the most extraordinary of all. Here, for the first time, he succeeded in fully releasing his obsessions in a work of art and creating, on a large scale, a painting of enduring power in which image and idea were completely fused. The composition consists of three main elements, a sleeping girl, an incubus or nightmare squatting on her belly, and the head of a horse peering through the curtains with wildly staring eyes. A table which stands at the foot of the bed carries a tray, a couple of jars and a dressing mirror. The three figures have a long history in the visual arts and the conception of the work itself is dependent on various current and complex attitudes to the subconscious mind. But its explicit meaning is immediately apparent.

As in most of Fuseli's works, the drawing is fluent and vigorous, but the colour leaves something to be desired. In this respect, his lack of technical training was always to be apparent. A contemporary (Leigh Hunt) remarked that his colouring 'was a sort of livid green, like brass diseased', and later R. D. S. Redgrave referred to it as 'honey and treacle'. In *The Nightmare* the curtain behind the scene is a dark theatrical red, the incubus brownish, the girl is clad in virginal white and lies on a fan-shaped shawl or coverlet of salmon pink and lemon yellow with thin grey stripes. It might well be supposed that Fuseli, like some Neo-classical painters, disdained colour as 'deceptive': but this would be mistaken. He claimed that he had courted and would continue to court colour as a lover courts a disdainful mistress. Haydon once saw him adding a terrible smear of Prussian blue to a flesh tint while remarking: 'By Gode dat's a fine purple! It's very like Correggio by Gode.' And to his pupils Fuseli expounded his method of painting with endearing frankness: 'First I sits myself down. Then I work myself up. Then I throw in my darks. Then I pulls out my lights.'[28]

According to Knowles, his first biographer, Fuseli had never used oil colours until he was twenty-five. 'And he was so inattentive to these materials that during his life he took no pains in their choice and manipulation. To set a palette, as artists usually do, was with him out of the question; he used many of his colours in a dry, powdered state, and rubbed them up with his pencil [i.e., brush] only, sometimes in oil alone, which he used largely, at others with the addition of a little spirit of turpentine, and not infrequently in gold size.' The technique of painting in oils was in fact the only part of Fuseli's education that had in any way been neglected.

2. Dreams and Nightmares

'An original enters early on reputation', wrote Edward Young in 1759. 'Fame fond of new glories sounds her trumpet in triumph at her birth.'[29] Few late–eighteenth–century artists were more anxious to hear those trumpet notes than Fuseli, and there can be little doubt that he chose to paint *The Nightmare* for exhibition at the Royal Academy partly, if not solely, in order to demonstrate his 'originality' and thereby bring himself prominently before the public. It should not be supposed that either in this aim or in his choice of subject matter, he was at odds with his time. The doctrine of 'originality' was written into the aesthetic theory of the late eighteenth century no less prominently than the now better known doctrine of 'imitation': and although Fuseli's subject was certainly rather unusual, his attitude to it – to the subconscious in general and to nightmares in particular – was highly characteristic of his time.

Dream pictures had, of course, been frequently painted by earlier artists. Fuseli's differs from them not only in representing a nightmare (a particular type of bad dream) but also in attempting to convey what is felt rather than what is 'seen' by the dreamer and in illustrating a general rather than a particular individual experience. Thus, his painting reflects both his contemporaries' interest in sensation, as the key to human understanding, and their demand that a work of art should have universal significance.

Most earlier dream pictures had had a literary or historical programme as, for example, *Jacob's Dream* [14] or *The Dream of Constantine* or *Hecuba's Dream*. But such dreams, which intimate future events, might equally well be described as visions, and in paintings of them the dreamer was generally shown asleep with the

14. *Jacob's Dream*, c. 1605–8.
L. Carracci

15. *Hecuba's Dream*, 1538-9.
Giulio Romano

dream figures around him – the latter being represented no less substantially than the former. In the famous *Dream of Constantine* in the Vatican, for example, supposed in Fuseli's day to be the work of Raphael but now assigned to Giulio Romano, the Emperor is shown standing and confronting the vision with a glassy-eyed stare. In *Hecuba's Dream*, on the other hand, Giulio Romano did suggest some distinction between the conspicuously 'solid flesh' of the dreamer and the insubstantiality of the winged figure warning her of the fall of Troy [15]. Fuseli adopted this system of dream representation for his drawing illustrating *Richard III*, V, 3 – the scene in which the ghosts of Henry VI, the Duke of Clarence, the two princes and others visit the sleeping king [16]. The king lies naked while round him move the ghosts like grey ectoplasmic presences.

16. *Richard III visited by Ghosts*, 1777. J. H. Fuseli

17. *Garrick as Richard III*, c. 1746. W. Hogarth

A more advanced and enlightened interpretation of the same scene may lie behind Hogarth's painting of it [17]. This is, of course, a portrait – of Garrick playing Richard – and Hogarth may not have intended it to be understood as a dream picture. If he did he was much in advance of his time. (It was painted some thirty-five years before Fuseli's *Nightmare*.) However, the picture may be interpreted in two different ways. The various ghosts in Shakespeare's play are not represented and Richard – or Garrick – stares out of the canvas directly at us; but are we intended to suppose that Richard sees the ghosts and that they are somewhere between the picture plane and us, or are we intended to suppose that Richard sees them only in his mind's eye? The latter interpretation would be a rationalization of Shakespeare's scene quite typical of the later eighteenth century when the belief in ghosts had been dispelled and the notion that dreams might foretell the future discountenanced – so that the figures of Henry VI, the Duke of Clarence, the two young princes and others who appear to Richard while he sleeps could be accepted only as fantasies produced by his 'coward conscience'.

But there had been another, rarer and more puzzling type of dream representation of which the classic examples are two engravings, both generally described as 'the Dream of Raphael', one by Giorgio Ghisi and the other by Marcantonio Raimondi.[30] The former shows a brooding central figure, who looks more like Michelangelo than Raphael, surrounded by a very large number of birds, beasts and reptiles, both real and fabulous, the majority of which seem to be devils. In Marcantonio's print two naked women are shown lying asleep beside a lake or stream beyond which figures may be seen escaping from a burning building. At the feet of the women there are four monstrous creatures composed of parts of the bodies of fish, reptiles and insects [18]. No satisfactory explanation has ever been found for either of these prints. But the monsters in that by Marcantonio have a classical ancestry of some importance. In the very first lines of *De Arte Poetica*, Horace wrote – I quote from the mid-eighteenth-century translation of Sir Philip Francis:

Suppose a painter to a human head
Should join a horse's neck, and wildly spread
The various plumage of the feather'd kind
O'er limbs of different beasts absurdly join'd;
Or if he gave to view a beauteous maid
Above the waist with every charm array'd
Should a foul fish her lower parts enfold,
Would you not laugh such pictures to behold?
Such is the book, that, like a sick man's dreams,
Varies all shapes, and mixes all extremes.

This is probably the source for Dürer's remark, 'If a person wants to create the stuff that dreams are made of, let him freely mix all sorts of creatures'; and it almost certainly inspired Goya's famous print *The Sleep of Reason Produces Monsters*[31] [49]. In fact, these famous lines of Horace are, literally, the *locus classicus* for the depiction of dream monsters and as such had a vast progeny.

Both Ghisi's and Marcantonio's prints may have some connection with scenes of witchcraft – especially the former where the central figure appears to have conjured up the creatures that surround him. *Stregonerie* or witchcraft scenes became very popular in the seventeenth century when Salvator Rosa painted the best known examples of the genre. And, of course, witches and nightmares were intimately related in Central European folk-lore. Nevertheless, it seems unlikely that *Stregonerie* had any direct influence on Fuseli's *Nightmare*, certainly not Salvator Rosa's, for Fuseli had little opinion of him. 'Terrific and grand in his conceptions of inanimate nature, he was reduced to attempts of hiding by boldness of hand, his inability of exhibiting her impassioned, or in the dignity of character: his line is vulgar: his magic visions, less founded on principles of terror than on mythologic trash and caprice, are to the probable combinations of nature, what the paroxysms of a fever are to the flights of vigorous fancy.'[32] It would be interesting, however, to know if the echo of Horace in the last clause was intentional.

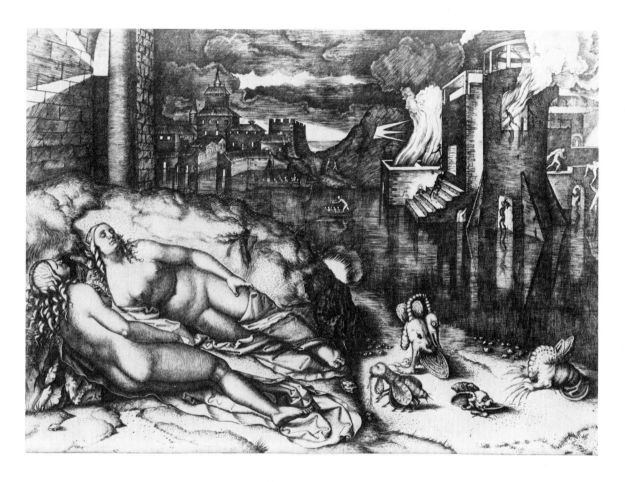

18. *The Dream of Raphael*,
c. 1506–10. Marcantonio Raimondi

Another sixteenth-century print generally known as *Der behexte Stallknecht* (The Bewitched Groom) by Hans Baldung Grien may represent either a scene of witchcraft or a dream or a combination of the two [19]. Here the main elements of Fuseli's *Nightmare* are already assembled – a victim, a horse and an evil spirit. The bewitched groom lies senseless on the floor with his legs towards us and his boldly foreshortened head pointing towards the frightened horse in the background. A threatening old woman holding a torch – is she a Witch or one of the Fates brandishing her spindle? – leans in at a window on the right. No one has as yet succeeded in unravelling the meaning of this disturbing print, but it seems more than

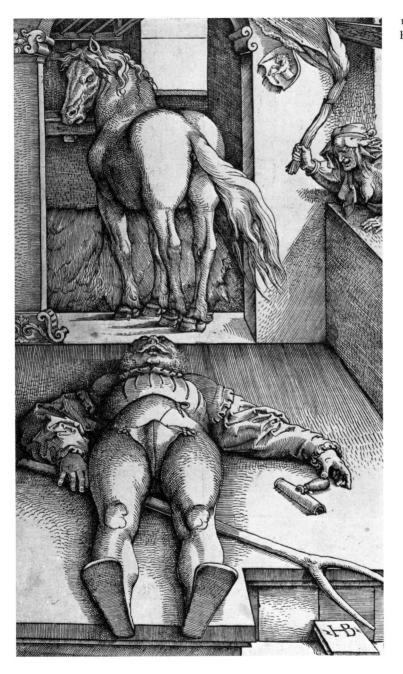

19. *The Bewitched Groom*, 1544.
Hans Baldung Grien

probable that the modern title is correct or at any rate that the subject is concerned with some popular belief about witchcraft. Fuseli doubtless knew this extraordinary print: but whereas Baldung Grien, delighting in his proficiency as a master of scientific perspective, seems to have wished to represent a real scene (or rather one that was real to him), Fuseli attempted in *The Nightmare* to depict a sensation. And, of course, in the two-and-a-half centuries that separated Baldung Grien from Fuseli, notions about witches and nightmares had been completely transformed among all but the most simple-minded.

Witches might easily be dismissed by the enlightened. But dreams, whether pleasant or nightmarish, provided the eighteenth-century thinker with a discomforting reminder that many common phenomena remained unexplained by the new philosophy. Up to the end of the eighteenth century, three distinct attitudes to dreams in general and nightmares in particular were current, all of them of ancient origin. First there was the folk or mythological interpretation: the belief that dreams were caused by spirits who flew about at night to trouble sleepers and occasionally to warn them of coming events. There was the allied Christian belief that dreams were visitations of angels or devils and that nightmares were the work of devils alone. Then there was the enlightened belief that dreams were caused by indigestion or some such physical disturbance.

The mythological interpretation found expression in folk tales, only occasionally breaking into literature, as in Edgar's song on the heath in *King Lear*, III, 4:

> *Saint Withold footed thrice the old;*
> *He met the nightmare and her nine fold;*
> *Bid her alight,*
> *And her troth plight,*
> *And, aroint thee, witch, aroint thee!*

But the Christian version of this interpretation, current in theological
literature from the Middle Ages onwards, survived even in educated
circles well into the eighteenth century. It was given further
currency by a curious little book published in London in 1764,
*A Philosophical Discourse on the Nature of Dreams by the Reverend
Mr Saalfeld. Minister of the Gospel at Lutzen-Sommern. Translated
from the German.* Saalfeld refers to 'spiritual beings without us . . .
Angels . . . Devils . . . Both of them may act on our soul, and on our
body, excite thoughts, and consequently also cause dreams.' And,
groping towards a description of a nightmare, he remarked 'that
we often dream of indifferent things, but at last the dream ends in
some extraordinary terror or fright . . . ' Saalfeld was not, however,
uninfluenced by more straightforward medical explanations and,
like less credulous writers of his time, mentions that 'frightful
dreams' tend to come when the sleeper is lying on his back or on his
left side.

Whether or not Fuseli had read Saalfeld's book, he must have
been well aware of the religious attitude it expressed, as well as of the
medical explanations of nightmares which soon passed into – and
still survive in – the repertory of old wives' tales. These rationalistic
explanations began in antiquity and recur in later writings. Burton,
for example, says that bad dreams may be caused by eating hare
or venison.[33] Even in the early nineteenth century Allan Cunningham thought it worth mentioning that Fuseli was said to have
'supped on raw pork chops that he might dream his picture of the
nightmare'.[34] But even if the phenomena of dreaming could be so
simply explained, the significance of the dreams themselves
presented very much more difficult problems to the philosopher.
Indeed dreams began to attain considerable importance in theories
of knowledge and sensation.

Hobbes raised the essential issues in the second chapter of
Leviathan.

'The imaginations of them that sleep, are those we call *Dreams.*
And these also (as all other Imaginations) have been before, either

totally, or by parcells in the Sense. And because in sense, the Brain, and Nerves, which are the necessary Organs of sense, are so benummed in sleep, as not easily to be moved by the action of Externall Objects, there can happen in sleep, no Imagination; and therefore no Dreame, but what proceeds from the agitation of the inward parts of mans body; which inward parts, for the connexion they have with the Brayn, and other Organs, when they be distempered, do keep the same in motion; whereby the Imaginations there formerly made, appear as if a man were waking; saving that the Organs of Sense being now benummed, so as there is no new object, which can master and obscure them with a more vigorous impression, a Dreame must needs be more cleare, in this silence of sense, than are our waking thoughts. And hence it cometh to passe, that it is a hard matter, and by many thought impossible to distinguish exactly between Sense and Dreaming . . . And seeing dreames are caused by the distemper of some of the inward parts of the Body; divers distempers must needs cause different Dreams. And hence it is, that lying cold breedeth Dreams of Feare, and raiseth the thought and Image of some fearfull object (the motion from the brain to the inner parts and from the inner parts to the Brain being reciprocall).'

To dreams he attributed a major role in the rise of superstitions.

‘From this ignorance of how to distinguish Dreams, and other strong Fancies, from Vision and Sense [he continued] did arise the greatest part of the Religion of the Gentiles in time past, that worshipped Satyres, Fawnes, Nymphs, and the like; and nowadayes the opinion that rude people have of Fayries, Ghosts, and Goblins; and of the power of Witches.'[35]

He took up the origin of belief in ghosts and spirits again in chapter 12 where, writing of ancient authors, he remarked:

‘And for the matter, or substance of the Invisible Agents, so fancyed; they could not by naturall cogitation, fall upon any other conceipt, but that it was the same with that of the Soule of man; and that the Soule of man, was of the same substance, with that which appeareth in a Dream, to one that sleepeth; or in a Looking-glasse, to one that is awake; which, men not knowing that such apparitions are nothing else but creatures of the Fancy, think to be reall, and externall Substances; and therefore call them Ghosts . . . '[36]

Several of these notions – and also the image of the looking-glass – were taken up by Locke in that cornerstone of enlightened thought, the *Essay Concerning Human Understanding*. Arguing against those who believed that the soul is always thinking (though 'methinks, every drowsy Nod shakes their Doctrine') and that dreams are its thoughts, he pointed out that some people cannot remember their dreams. 'To think often, and never to retain it so much as one moment, is a very useless sort of thinking', he declared. 'And the Soul, in such a state of thinking, does very little if at all, excel that of a looking-glass, which constantly receives variety of Images, or *Ideas*, but retains none: they disappear and vanish and there remain no foot-steps of them; the Looking-glass is never the better of such *ideas*, nor the Soul for such Thoughts.'[37] Passing to the subject of dreams, he wrote: 'The Dreams of sleeping Men are, as I take it, all made up of the waking Man's Ideas, though for the most part odly put together. 'Tis strange if the Soul has Ideas of its own, that it derived not from Sensation or Reflection (as it must have, if it thought before it receiv'd any impressions from the Body) that it should never in its private thinking (so private that Man himself perceives it not) retain any of them, the very moment it wakes out of them, and then make the man glad with new discoveries.'[38]

These passages summarize the Enlightenment view of dreams – of their causes and their meaning, or rather their 'significance', if any – which were current in Fuseli's day; and they indicate clearly enough why his *Nightmare* aroused such enormous interest when it was first exhibited. It was obviously painted by an artist fully aware of contemporary theories about the conscious and unconscious. His depiction in no way conflicts with Locke and his conception of knowledge derived from experience or sensation and according to whom the human mind or memory merely 'freewheels', as it were, in a dream. In Fuseli's *Nightmare* the horse and the incubus are not 'seen' by the sleeper: they are symbols of the terror and suffocating oppression which she feels. (She is shown, significantly, in a position from which she could not see either, even were her eyes open.) Moreover, these symbols are drawn from 'waking thoughts', from folk-lore and literature.

It is tempting to go one step further. No one of Fuseli's upbringing and range of interests would have been unaware of the writings of Hobbes and Locke. Might he have intended, by placing a looking-glass on the bedside-table in *The Nightmare*, to make a specific allusion to one or both of the passages I have quoted? Of course, looking-glasses frequently appear in Fuseli's works: as early as 1765 he referred in a letter to a monkey, toilet-table and mirror in some work on which he was then engaged.[39] But he normally used them, whether in the drawing of Ezzelin Bracciaferro [13] or in his numerous near-pornographic studies of women, to provide a mirror image of the back (or more usually the front) of the main figure or figures. In *The Nightmare* the looking-glass shows no image, though it is placed in such a way that it could reflect the figure of the incubus squatting on the sleeper's stomach. The mirror was also the symbol of the mimetic theory of the arts: and it may not be too far-fetched to suggest that Fuseli had this in mind as well. By including in *The Nightmare* a looking-glass which in fact reflects nothing, he seems to tell us that the painting faithfully records an image which would otherwise fade away, and also that the nocturnal visitation depicted is a mere figment of the imagination.

A nightmare is, however, a special type of dream. Dr Johnson's definition is of some importance: 'NIGHTMARE (*night* and according to Temple, *mara*, a spirit that, in the northern mythology, was related to torment or suffocate sleepers). A morbid oppression in the night, resembling the pressure of weight upon the breast.' This serves as a reminder that in English at this period the nightmare had no etymological connection with a female horse. In Fuseli's picture the creature squatting on the sleeper's stomach is the nightmare, not – as many recent writers have assumed – the horse. Johnson cites the passage from *King Lear* and also Dr Arbuthnot's statement that 'the forerunners of an apoplexy are dulness, drowsiness, vertigoes, tremblings, oppressions in sleep and night-mares'. For the physical phenomenon eighteenth-century writers seem, however, to have preferred the term incubus which Johnson defined simply as a nightmare, quoting a passage from Sir John Floyer (a doctor who was practising in Lichfield when he was a boy and on whose advice he was taken to London to be 'touched for the evil' by Queen Anne). 'The incubus', Floyer stated, 'is an inflation of the membranes of the stomach, which hinders the motion of the diaphragm, lungs, and pulse, with a sense of a weight oppressing the breast.'

Explanations such as Floyer's were certainly rational but they hardly helped those who suffered from persistent nightmares. One of these was Dr John Bond who wrote the first book in English on the subject, *An Essay on the Incubus, or Nightmare*, published in 1753. His account of the phenomenon is vivid.

'The Nightmare generally seizes people sleeping on their backs, and often begins with frightful dreams, which are soon succeeded by a difficult respiration, a violent oppression of the breast, and a total privation of voluntary motion. In this agony they sigh, groan, utter indistinct sounds, and remain in the jaws of death, till, by the utmost efforts of nature, or some external assistance, they escape out of that dreadful torpid state. As soon as they shake off that vast oppression, and are able to move the body, they are affected with a strong Palpitation, great Anxiety, Languor, and Uneasiness; which symptoms gradually abate, and are gradually succeeded by the pleasing reflection of having escaped some imminent danger.'

Bond goes on to say, 'I have often been so much oppressed by this enemy of rest, that I would have given ten thousand worlds like this for some Person that would either pinch, shake or turn me off my back; and I have been so much afraid of its intolerable insults, that I have slept in a chair all night, rather than give it an opportunity of attacking me in a horizontal position.' Ascribing nightmares to a complication in the blood circulation aggravated by lying on the back, he was able to derive a wholly rational conclusion from his study. 'Are not these monstrous dreams', he asked, 'intended as a stimulus to rouse the sentient principle in us, that we might alter the position of the body, and by that means avoid the approaching danger?' Some years later Kant said much the same thing in *Anthropologie* where he claimed that the nightmare was a beneficent process making the sleeper aware of the danger to his circulation from lying in a constrained posture.[40]

Such notions about dreams and nightmares were generally accepted among the more intelligent in the mid eighteenth century. That Fuseli shared them seems more than probable, especially when they are compared with the very different theories developed towards the end of the century, even by writers who were his close contemporaries. Georg Christoph Lichtenberg, who was only one year younger than Fuseli, was perhaps one of the most interesting of these. Though he agreed with the enlightened that dreams were not supernatural visitations and did not foretell the future, he became fascinated by their content. 'Instead of bringing our specious wisdom and zeal into play against the interpretation of dreams,' he wrote in his notebook, 'we should really restrict our criticism to dream books. I know from irrefutable experience that dreams lead to self-knowledge.' And, again, with a sly dig at Lavater: 'If people would recount their dreams truthfully, one might divine character more correctly from dreams than from faces.'[41] Extracted and isolated out of context, these passages might seem to anticipate Freud. But Lichtenberg developed no system for the analysis of dreams. His outlook was closer to that of the German romantics and especially to G. H. von Schubert. 'The road behind us is dark', Schubert wrote in 1808: 'only occasionally is it lit up by dreams of a remarkable clarity and intensity, dreams which appear to be related one to the other but which have no connection with present, everyday existence. In such dreams, and more especially in the profound mystery of magnetic attraction and repulsion, we must often see and acknowledge memories of a state of life which has gone before.'[42] In his book on the *Symbolik des Traumes* (1814) Schubert worked this notion out more fully, arguing that the soul approached Eternity more readily in dreams than was possible for a mere waking human being. As a doctor of medicine, Schubert was somewhat exceptional in holding such views, typical though they are of the romantic poet. For here we are not far from Shelley's claim that

> *gleams of a remoter world*
> *Visit the soul in sleep.*

But we have passed a long way beyond Fuseli's *Nightmare*.

3. The Female Victim

In literature and especially folk legend, the nightmare had strong sexual connotations. Thus, Mercutio in the famous 'Queen Mab' speech in *Romeo and Juliet*, I, 4:

> *This is the hag, when maids lie on their backs,*
> *That presses them, and learns them first to bear,*
> *Making them women of good carriage:*

The same image was employed by Michael Drayton:

> *Mab his merry queen by night,*
> *Bestrides young folks that lie upright,*
> *In elder times the mare that hight,*
> *Which plagues them out of measure.*

Both passages are examples of a light-hearted, Elizabethan bawdy; but the proneness of women to suffer from nightmares was more seriously noted – and explained. The great Swiss physician and philosopher, Paracelsus, had said that the menstrual flux engendered phantoms in the air, making convents seminaries of Nightmares.[43] And Burton took up the notion in *The Anatomy of Melancholy* (a book 'revived', thanks to Johnson's praise, in Fuseli's time). 'Maids, nuns and widows', Burton remarked, were particularly subject to 'terrible dreams in the night', a symptom of melancholy which could be cured by marriage.[44] Hobbes was later to note how the ancients had 'attributed their pollutions to Incubi and Succubi'.[45]

The connections between nightmares, 'pollutions' and the devil led, however, to tragic results. Burton remarked that some denied 'that the devil hath any carnal copulation with women, that the devil takes no pleasure in such facts, they be mere phantasies, all such relations of incubi, succubi, lies and tales.' But he cited St

Augustine and others who upheld the belief.[46] It was certainly widespread in the Middle Ages. A manuscript illumination in *L'Histoire dou Merline* of about 1280 (Bibliothèque Nationale, Paris), shows the devil as incubus in bed with a woman, and in the sixteenth and seventeenth centuries literally thousands of women were burnt as witches after confessing to nocturnal sexual intercourse with the devil. Nor were such confessions invariably extracted under torture. The unfortunate Françoise Fontaine, for instance, stated that she was visited at night by a huge black figure who 'jetteit quelque chose dans son ventre qui estoit froid comme glace, qui venoit jusques au dessus de l'estomac et des tétins de ladite respondant'. As Professor Hugh Trevor-Roper has pointed out, confessions such as this seemed genuine to those who made them and 'we can hardly blame the inquisitors for supposing them to be genuine too. What was "subjective reality" to the penitent was "objective reality" to the confessor.'[47]

In the sceptical atmosphere of the mid eighteenth century, Dr John Bond opened the essay from which I have already quoted by dismissing all such medieval aberrations. 'I have not introduc'd anything in this Essay that did not appear serious or probable', he wrote. 'I have therefore omitted an inquiry into the origins of many old epithets and quaint names commonly given to this Disorder: such as Hag-riding, Wizard-pressing, Mare-riding, Witch dancing &c. nor did I think it requisite to mention particularly the curious charms adapted to each superstitious name.' Nevertheless, he went on to provide case histories of girls who suffered from nightmares – together, of course, with wholly rational explanations of them.

'A young lady of a tender, lax habit, about fifteen, before the Menses appeared, was seized with a fit of this Disease [a Nightmare] and groan'd so miserably that she awoke her Father, who was sleeping in the next room. He arose, ran into her chamber, and found her lying on her Back, with the Blood gushing plentifully out of her Mouth and Nose. When he shook her, she recover'd and told him, that she thought some great heavy Man came to her bedside, and, without farther ceremony, stretched himself upon her. She had been heard moaning in sleep several nights before; but, the next day after she imagin'd herself oppress'd by that Man, she had a copious eruption of the Menses, which, for that time, remov'd all her complaints.'

He also recounted the story of a 'robust servant girl, about eighteen years old'. She was 'severely oppressed with the Nightmare, two or three nights before every eruption of the Menses, and used to groan so loudly as to awake her Fellow-servant, who always shook or turn'd her on her Side, by which means she recover'd. She was thus afflicted periodically with it until she took a bed fellow of a different sex, and bore children.'

The sleeper lying on her back – as in Fuseli's painting – is, of course, in a normally receptive sexual attitude. But a man might also, as Burton pointed out, be ridden by a hag in the night. And although he plays a masculine part, his role is passive. The woman who wishes to seduce a man and employs magic to enter his room while he is sleeping is a familiar figure in folk tales. One of them – from the Wuppenau in Switzerland, significantly enough – is quoted by Ernest Jones. The 'mara penetrates through the keyhole into the bed-chamber in the guise of a steed, lays her fore-hoofs on the sleeper's breast, and with glowing eyes stares at him in the most alarming fashion.'

The late eighteenth-century interest in all forms of ancient legend led to the collection and recording of folk tales and super-stitions, many of them of a nightmarish kind, and accounts for the extraordinary popularity of such books as the *Viaggio in Dalmazia* published by Alberto Fortis in Venice in 1774 (translated into German in 1776 and into both English and French two years later), which described in some detail the popular beliefs still surviving in Dalmatia. 'The Moldo Wallachians believe in witches and goblins and spells and nocturnal apparitions so strongly as if they had seen their practical effects in a thousand cases', Fortis wrote. 'They also believe in the very real existence of vampires and

attribute to them as in Transylvania the sucking of blood of girls.'
As this work first appeared while Fuseli was in Italy, and a translation was published in Berne the year he returned to Switzerland, it
seems likely that he read it or at any rate heard of it. And he may also
have come across the even more curious reply to Fortis published
by Giovanni Lovrich in Venice in 1776; *Osservazioni sopra diversi
pezzi del viaggio in Dalmazia del Signor Abate Alberto Fortis.*
Lovrich included a whole section on nightmares or 'Morre' or
'Smarre', and the closely related vampires.

'The incubus of the ancients is called a Morra, from the Mor-
lacchi. This is a witch who by night sucks blood from people of all
ages, not only young girls.' The male Morra attacked women while
the female of the species preyed on men, and those on whom it
descended felt that they were being stifled. 'Ancient physicians
defined the incubus as a dream of impure coitus with the devil. But
Reason teaches that high blood pressure, or a position of lying in
bed with the head thrown too far back may make the sleeper feel a
want of breath as if he is being suffocated. It is hardly surprising
that this phenomenon, which occurs between waking and sleeping,
has given birth to the superstition of the *Morre, Smarre,* or *Pesaroli,*
as the Italians commonly call it.'

In *The Nightmare* the sexual significance of the incubus is plain
enough – Fuseli was to repeat its monstrous form to represent the
most libidinous of Shakespeare's characters, Caliban [20]. But the
horse on which it has apparently ridden into the room is also a very
ancient masculine sexual symbol: and it was also, as Jung has
demonstrated, frequently associated with the devil and there was
an intimate connection between the devil, nightmares and sex. 'Just
as the nightmare rides on the sleeper, so does the devil, and therefore,
it is said that those who have nightmares are ridden by the devil,'
he remarked. 'The devil, like all evil things, represents sexuality.'[48]

But is the horse peering so ominously through the curtains in
Fuseli's *Nightmare* a stallion or a mare? As we have already seen,
the word nightmare had no etymological connection with a female

Act 1. TEMPEST. Sc. 2.

Fuseli del. Bromley sculp.

_____ *Miranda sleeps.*

Prosp. { *Come away, servant, come: I am ready now:*
approach, my Ariel; come.

Publish'd by F & C. Rivington London Jan 1. 1803.

horse: it derives from the same root as Mara or Smarra. On a print of the picture published in 1783, however, the following lines by Erasmus Darwin were engraved:

> *So on his NIGHTMARE through the evening fog*
> *Flits the squab fiend o'er fen, and lake and bog;*
> *Seeks some love-wildered Maid with sleep oppress'd,*
> *Alights, and grinning sits upon her breast.*

It is recorded that there was no horse in Fuseli's first sketch for his painting, and a drawing which omits the horse has been associated with this initial stage in the development of the composition [21].

21. *The Nightmare.*
Anonymous, after J. H. Fuseli

(This drawing does not appear to me to be in Fuseli's hand, though it may be a copy after a lost original, see Appendix I.) As Darwin was a friend of Fuseli, it has been suggested that he may have persuaded him to include the horse's head so that the picture would illustrate his lines.[49] However, the reverse is equally possible. The completed painting may well have inspired Darwin's lines and the dominating position of the horse may have led him, mistakenly, to identify the nightmare with it rather than with the incubus or 'squab fiend', as he called it. Fuseli's painting would thus have been indirectly responsible, through Darwin, for the still common misunderstanding of the word 'nightmare' and its erroneous connection with a 'mare' or female horse.

The lines quoted above come from Darwin's long didactic poem, *The Loves of the Plants*, which was not fully published until 1789. The passage continues:

> – Such as of late by *FUSELI'S* poetic eye;
> Whose daring tints, with *SHAKESPEAR's* happiest grace,
> Gave to the airy phantom form and place. –
> Back o'er her pillow sinks her blushing head,
> Her snow-white limbs hang helpless from the bed;
> While with quick sighs, and suffocative breath,
> Her interrupted heart-pulse swims in death.
> – Then shrieks of captur'd towns and widow's tears,
> Pale lovers stretch'd upon their blood-stain'd biers,
> The headlong precipice that thwarts her flight,
> The trackless desert, the cold starless night,
> And stern-eyed Murderer with his knife behind,
> In dread succession agonise her mind.
> O'er her fair limbs convulsive tremors fleet;
> Start in her hands and struggle in her feet;
> In vain to scream with quivering lips she tries,
> And strains in palsy'd lids her tremulous eyes;
> In vain she wills to run, fly, swim, walk, creep;

The WILL presides not in the bower of SLEEP.
– On her fair bosom sits the Demon-Ape,
Erect, and balances his bloated shape;
Rolls in their marble orbs his Gorgon-eyes
And drinks with leathern ears her tender cries.

It is perhaps idle to speculate on whether the prominence given to the word 'erect', three lines from the end of the passage, was intentional or inadvertent. But no matter what Darwin wrote about the subject of the dream, there can be little doubt that the girl in Fuseli's painting is experiencing an imaginary sexual assault.

This brings us to what is perhaps the innermost layer of meaning in *The Nightmare*. On his last visit to Zurich, Fuseli fell deeply in love with Lavater's niece, Anna Landolt. Because he was too poor to marry her, he did not declare his feelings. But he did not hesitate to pour them out in poems and in letters to Lavater and to others who knew the girl. 'Is she in Zurich now?' he asked Lavater on 16 June 1779. 'Last night I had her in bed with me – tossed my bedclothes hugger-mugger – wound my hot and tight-clasped hands about her – fused her body and her *soul* together with my own – poured into her my spirit, breath and strength. Anyone who touches her now commits adultery and incest! She is *mine*, and I am *hers*. And have her I will . . . What God or Nature hath joined, let no man – let no business-man sunder.' (The last remark presumably refers to the merchant whom Anna Landolt was shortly to marry.) Is it too bold a conjecture, as Professor Janson has asked, to see the sleeper in Fuseli's painting as a projection of Anna Landolt 'with the incubus demon taking the place of the artist himself'? Examination of the first version of *The Nightmare* has disclosed an unfinished portrait of a young woman painted on the back of the canvas [22]. May this not represent Anna Landolt?[50] Whether or not it does, and whether or not *The Nightmare* was inspired by his hopeless passion for her, the painting is deeply impregnated with Fuseli's obsessive, ambivalent sexual feelings. It is almost his case-book.

22. *Portrait of a Lady, c.* 1779.
J. H. Fuseli

23. *Brunhilde and Gunther*, 1807. J. H. Fuseli

Throughout his life, Fuseli was obsessed with the battle of the sexes which he generally represented as a distinctly unequal conflict [9]. There is nothing tender or sentimental about his many embracing figures: they struggle with a strenuous ardour more appropriate to the palestra than to the alcove. Flexing their great sinews, the men wrap preternaturally muscular limbs around curiously slippery, boneless, sometimes almost reptilian, female bodies. Occasionally he allowed the woman to dominate and she is shown relishing the discomfiture of a hero – Brunhilde smiling at Gunther strung up from the ceiling [23], Delilah visiting Samson in prison,[51] and, of course, Lady Macbeth. His response to, or perhaps one should say respect for, the triumphant dominating female even coloured his attitude to the art of the past. He praised Guercino's women who 'dart insidious fire': but, he wrote, 'the women of Michael Angelo are the sex.'[52]

Generally, however, man triumphs in Fuseli's sexual fantasies and woman is submissive, if not completely vanquished. As we have already seen, in *Ezzelin Bracciaferro* – for which he had made a preliminary drawing in Zurich in 1779 just as he was discovering his passion for Anna Landolt – he depicted a heroic figure musing over the prostrate corpse of a gagged woman [13]. Writing of Domenichino's women, he remarked approvingly that 'their expression is poised between pure helpless virginity and sainted ectasy.'[53] This might lead one to suppose that his ideal of femininity was the nun. But no. In a letter he wrote to Knowles in 1809 he declared, 'your account of the Nunneries you have visited confirms Hamlet's verdict: "Frailty thy name is woman!" How self-contradictory that the "animal of beauty", as Dante calls women, should exchange her claims to social admiration and pleasure, and the substantial charms of life, for the sterile embraces of a crucifix or some withered sister, by the dim glimmer of cloistered light – lost to hope, and marked by oblivion for her own! Tyranny, deception, and most of all, that substitute for every other want, "the undistinguished space of woman's will", can account for such phenomena.'[54] 'The words reflect an anti-Catholic attitude which had been prevalent for several centuries. But one may wonder if Fuseli remembered Paracelsus' description of convents as 'seminaries of nightmares'.

In his *Aphorisms* Fuseli wrote, 'Female affection is in proportion to the impression of superiority in the object. Woman fondles, pities, despises and forgets what is below her; she values, bears and wrangles with her equal; she adores what is above her.'[55] For him women appear to have been essentially instruments for the pleasure of men – the pleasure probably including what were later to be called sadism and masochism, hence his response to the virago. In drawing after drawing he represented women who are unmistakably whores – décolletées, and with fantastic coiffures, ogling or often coquetting before their mirrors [24]. And many of his more overtly erotic drawings show two women who assist in satisfying the heroic lust of one man. Many of the latter are indeed pornographic, in the true sense of the word, and make a significant departure from the tradition established by Giulio Romano in his 'postures'. Fuseli may even have hinted at such orgies by combining one female with two male elements in *The Nightmare*.

'The Engines in Fuseli's Mind are Blasphemy, lechery and blood,' wrote B. R. Haydon in a petulant moment. 'His women are all whores, and men all banditti. They are whores not from the love of pleasure but from a hatred, a malignant spite against virtue, and his men are not villains from a daring desire or wish, but a licentious turbulence.'[56] This may somewhat overstate the case, but there can be no doubt that a great proportion of Fuseli's work appealed to his contemporaries, and still appeals mainly on account of its implied and often overt erotic overtones.

In contrast to the violence of his erotic fantasies, Fuseli's own private life seems to have been distinctly tame. In 1788 he married Sophia Rawlins, who had been an artist's model and was as inferior to him in social position as in intellect. Contemporaries say that she was a good wife to him and worshipped his genius, but she bore him no children. Shortly after they married, Mary Wollstonecraft

24. *Lady Seated at her Dressing Table, c.* 1780. J. H. Fuseli

became infatuated with Fuseli. 'I find that I cannot live without the satisfaction of seeing him and conversing with him daily,' she told Sophia who immediately and sensibly forbade her the house. She wrote soon afterwards her *Vindication of the Rights of Women* – a book with which Fuseli can have had little sympathy.[57]

Fuseli was a man of very short stature – hence perhaps his aggressiveness as well as his admiration for the colossal. Leigh Hunt, who met him in the early years of the nineteenth century, described him as 'a small man, with energetic features and a white head of hair. Our host's daughter, then a little girl, used to call him the white-headed lion. He combed his hair up from the forehead; and as his whiskers were large, his face was set in a kind of hairy frame, which, in addition to the fierceness of his look, really gave him an aspect of that sort. Otherwise, his features were rather sharp than round. He would have looked much like a military officer, if his face, besides its real energy, had not affected more. There was the same defect in it as in his pictures. Conscious of not having all the strength he wished, he endeavoured to make up for it by violence and pretension.' Hunt also said that 'he painted horrible pictures, as children tell horrible stories; and was frightened by his own lay figures'.[58] Was he perhaps striving after a virility he did not possess? Coleridge may have guessed what the situation was, and said no less than he intended, when he referred to Fuseli's 'vigorous impotence'.[59]

4. The Judicious Adoption of Figures in Art

If the conception of *The Nightmare* was more typical of its period and less in advance of it than might be supposed, the pictorial language in which Fuseli clothed it was equally so. Indeed, he drew more heavily on the art of the past, especially of the classical past, than is at all apparent. For though he strove after 'originality' he in no way differed from his contemporaries in his opinion about 'imitation'. As he remarked in his third Academy lecture, 'Horace, the most judicious of critics, when treating of the use of poetic words, tells his pupils that the adoption of an old word, rendered novel by a skilful construction with others, will entitle the poet to the praise of original diction. The same will be granted to the judicious adoption of figures in art.'[60] Here he was of course in full agreement with the writings of Sir Joshua Reynolds, the only artistic theorist whom he consistently praised: and it was to Reynolds that he owed his first and largest debt for the figure in *The Nightmare*.

In 1781, while Fuseli was working on *The Nightmare*, Reynolds exhibited his painting of *The Death of Dido* [25] at the Royal Academy. Fuseli already knew Reynolds well at this date and later revealed that he had frequently visited him in 1781 and watched him at work on this picture. Writing in 1803 about a collection of pictures by Reynolds on exhibition at the British Institution, he remarked of *The Death of Dido*: 'This is one of the few historic compositions anywhere, and perhaps a solitary one in this collection, of which the principal figure is the best and occupies the most

25. *The Death of Dido*, 1781. Sir Joshua Reynolds

conspicuous place. Riveted to supreme beauty in the jaws of death, we pay little attention to the subordinate parts. . . The writer of these observations has seen the progress of the work – if not daily, weekly – and knows the throes which it cost the author before it emerged into the beauty, assumed the shape, or was divided into the powerful masses of chiar'oscuro which strike us now; of colour it never had nor wants, more than it possesses now – a negative share.'[61] In this revealing passage – equally or more revealing about his own work than about that of Reynolds – Fuseli shows how deep an impression *The Death of Dido* had made on him, and a comparison of the two pictures leaves little doubt that he found inspiration in it for the figure of his sleeping girl.

26. *Sleeping Psyche*, 1528.
Giulio Romano

But Reynolds's Dido is herself a borrowing from the past. She is based on, indeed copied from, Giulio Romano's *Sleeping Psyche* [26] in the Sala di Psiche in the Palazzo del Tè at Mantua.[62] Fuseli may well have noted this painting when he visited Mantua on his way from Rome to Venice in 1772, and if he also visited the Palazzo Ducale in Mantua he could have seen another painting by Giulio Romano which may have influenced both Reynolds and himself – *Hecuba's Dream* [15].[63] The sofa on which the sleeping Hecuba lies has a post carved in the form of a horse's head, which may also be significant for an understanding of Fuseli's sources. Unlike both Dido and the girl in *The Nightmare*, Hecuba rests her head on her left arm – an ancient convention to indicate that the figure is asleep

27. *Ariadne*. Vatican Museum

28 *(right)*. *The Nightmare* (detail)

and not dead. Of the many antique statues which show a sleeping figure in this way the Vatican *Ariadne* [27] was probably the most famous in Giulio Romano's day and was still regarded as one of the outstanding masterpieces of ancient art in Fuseli's. Here, indeed, is yet another source for the girl in *The Nightmare* – especially the Frankfurt version where the crossed feet are exactly repeated [7].

The horse in *The Nightmare* [28] seems to have an artistic ancestry quite as remote as that of the sleeping figure. A number of sources have been proposed: the wild horses in a woodcut by Hans Baldung Grien [30][64] whose print of the bewitched groom has such strange affinities with Fuseli's painting, as we have already seen; the spirited and ferocious horses in engravings after Leonardo da Vinci's *Battle of the Standard* or *Battle of Anghiari*;[65] and the strange horse peering round a wall in the background of Veronese's *Venus and Mars* [29][66] which has unmistakably sexual overtones.

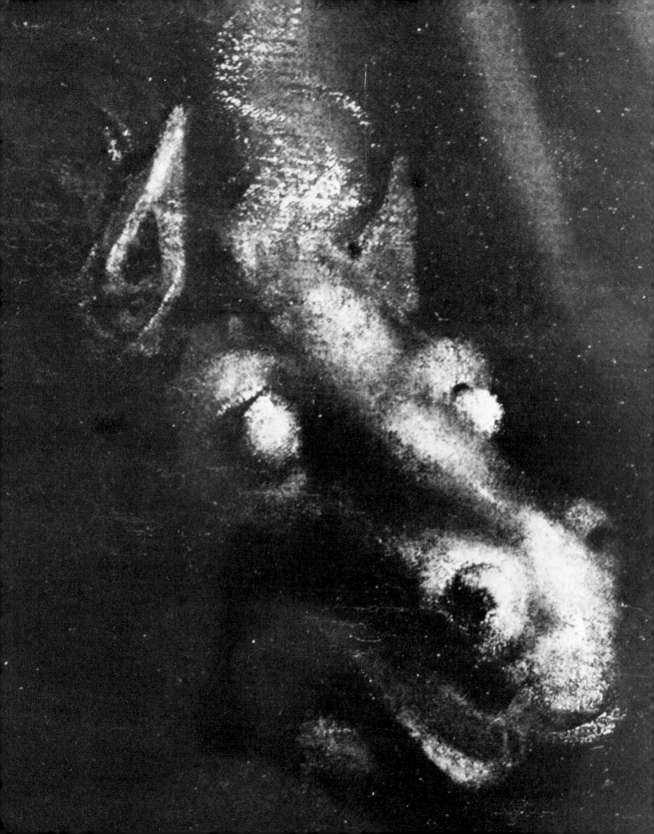

29 *(left)*. *Venus and Mars*, 1575–84. P. Veronese

30. *Wild Horses* (detail), 1534. Hans Baldung Grien

31 *(right)*. *The Horse Tamers* (detail), Piazza Quirinale, Rome

But the main source of inspiration must surely have been the famous group of horse-tamers in the Piazza Quirinale in Rome [31]. They were among the most famous of all classical antiquities – being thought to be by Phidias and identified as Castor and Pollux – and of course their colossal scale would have particularly recommended them to Fuseli.

That classical origins may be found for both the sleeping figure and the horse is not altogether surprising. The incubus itself however might seem to be essentially northern and non-classical both as an image and an idea [32]. Yet Erasmus Darwin's reference to its 'Gorgon eyes' is suggestive and tantalizing. Gorgons and grotesque figures of this kind were carved and modelled in antiquity and they were frequently painted on the pottery vases which Fuseli's

32. *The Nightmare* (detail)

33. Antique Silenus

34. *The Hunchbacked Beggar*,
3rd century B.C.

contemporaries called 'Etruscan'. Fuseli's incubus is reminiscent of several of these and also of some Silenus figures [33]. Another striking analogy is to be found in a small bronze statuette, now called the 'hunch-backed beggar', generally dated in the third century B.C. and assigned to Asia Minor [34].[67] Many versions of this exist: sometimes the figure holds a phallus, sometimes he plays a flute – symbolizing a phallus. But in each version the crouching posture, lascivious leer, and scrawny rounded backbone with its ribbed joints strikingly parallels Fuseli's incubus.

There can be little doubt that the three figures in *The Nightmare* had their origins in ancient art, which Fuseli 'rendered novel' by the way in which he combined them. For the furnishings – the stool and table (the bed is hardly visible) – he might similarly have gone to ancient sources, to paintings found at Pompeii and Herculaneum or to vase painting; or he might have used antique revival furniture of the type being made by fashionable cabinet-makers in England in the 1780s. But he did not. Instead, he depicted pieces which would have been quite obviously 'contemporary' – an upholstered stool and a mahogany table with curving legs in a simplified rococo manner.[68] In this way his *Nightmare* was presented, apparently with the most persuasive circumstantial detail, as a contemporary scene and subject – not as some fanciful mythological or literary one. Had he not succeeded in doing this so convincingly the painting would not have had the impact it did on the public.

5. *Impact and Repercussions*

When *The Nightmare* was exhibited in 1782, Horace Walpole described it as 'shocking'.[69] Yet less than twenty years earlier Walpole had turned one of his own dreams to good account in his novel *The Castle of Otranto*, which won immediate and widespread success, and contained such scenes of horror that Thomas Gray and his friends in Cambridge were 'afraid to go to bed o'nights'. There was, however, a fundamental difference between Walpole's and Fuseli's dreams. Walpole dreamed 'that I thought myself in an ancient castle (a very natural dream for a head filled like mine with Gothic story) and that on the upper bannisters of the staircase I saw a gigantic hand in armour.' He was, in other words, inspired by chivalric romances of the Middle Ages and the sixteenth century, so his dream was safely distanced from him and us in the medieval past. Fuseli's dream was of a very different type; and it was set insistently in the present. It was, perhaps, this contemporaneity and immediacy which shocked Walpole and others, for it seemed to involve them personally in the equivocal, lubricous sensations depicted. Walpole was no prude, but he had a proper respect for the conventions and such scenes as that depicted in *The Nightmare* required some mythological or other 'distancing' to render them acceptable in his eyes.

No painting quite like *The Nightmare* had previously been hung in an exhibition at the Royal Academy. It was difficult to classify: and this must also have puzzled and disturbed those who saw it then. It seemed to belong to none of the categories into which paintings were academically divided – history paintings, fancy pictures (what we now call genre pictures), portraits and landscapes.

35. *The Nightmare* (detail)

Its theme would have indicated classification as a fancy picture (a term which Fuseli disliked), but it was painted on the scale of a history painting and its 'modernity' connected it with a contemporary trend in history painting, established by two American painters in England, Benjamin West and John Singleton Copley. West's *Death of Wolfe* had shocked the public because the figures were in modern dress, as were those in Copley's alarmingly 'actual' *Brook Watson and the Shark*.

But Fuseli's painting was less close to these than to a number of renderings of horrific subjects, generally classified as history paintings, which enjoyed enormous popularity in late eighteenth-century England. Such pictures included Hogarth's *Satan, Sin and Death* of 1764, Reynolds's *Ugolino* and Alexander Runciman's *Satan Starting from the Touch of Ithuriel's Spear*, both exhibited in the Academy of 1773, James Barry's *Satan, Sin and Death* of about 1775 and, of course, various works by John Hamilton Mortimer which were described by the Shakespearian tag 'horrible imaginings' – the most notable being *Death on a Pale Horse* [36].[70] In the Royal Academy exhibition of 1782 – the year of *The Nightmare* – West's *Battle Between Michael and Satan*, Downman's *The Ghost of Clytemnestra Awakening the Furies* and Maria Cosway's *Eolus Raising a Storm* all seem to have answered the taste for horror. Yet, despite its obvious affinities with this type of painting, *The Nightmare* did not really belong among them.

In 1786 'Anthony Pasquin' made one of the characters in his scurrilous farce, *The Royal Academician*, say of Maria Cosway: 'She's as well acquainted with the sublime as the immortal EDMUND or the great FUSELI.' Surprising though it is to find Fuseli being named alongside Edmund Burke, especially in connection with the Sublime, this remark provides the clue as to how Fuseli himself would have categorized his painting.[71]

Fuseli set out his notions of the sublime fairly clearly in his third Academy lecture (delivered in 1801). 'Invention in its more specific sense receives its subjects from poetry or authenticated tradition,'

36. *Death on a Pale Horse*, 1784.
After J. H. Mortimer

he declared; 'they are *epic* or sublime, *dramatic* or impassioned, *historic* or circumscribed by truth. The first *astonishes*; the second *moves*, the third *informs*. The aim of the epic painter is to impress one general idea, one great quality of nature or mode of society, some great maxim, without descending to those subdivisions which the detail of character prescribes; he paints the elements with their own simplicity, height, depth, the vast, the grand, darkness, light, life, death, the past, the future; man, pity, love, joy, fear, terror, peace, war, religion, government; and the visible agents are only engines to force *one* irresistible idea upon the mind and fancy, as the machinery or Archimedes served only to convey *destruction* and the wheels of the watch serve only to tell *time*.'[72] In *The Nightmare* Fuseli had set out to create an epic or sublime painting of a modern subject. Every element in the picture is subservient to his one general idea.

Despite or because of its unusual, indeed 'shocking', nature, *The Nightmare* attracted a great deal of attention at the Royal Academy and an engraving issued the following year is said to have earned its publisher more than £500 (though Fuseli received only twenty guineas). Both variants and copies were called for (see Appendix I) – George Morland was among those who are said to have copied it[73] – but the most striking testimony to the impact which the picture made is provided by caricatures. Few, if any, English paintings of this period were so frequently travestied. (For a list of notable caricature versions see Appendix II.) Some of these are simple burlesques of the picture itself, but the majority use the composition as a basis for personal or political satire. The earliest, and perhaps the best, drawn by Rowlandson, has a burly nude Charles James Fox as the victim of both the dream and the print itself [3]. Issued during the election campaign of 1784 and entitled 'The Covent Garden Night Mare', it shows Fox with dice and dice box beside him, dreaming of defeat. Fox was again shown as the victim in a caricature of 1799 published in the *Anti-Jacobin Review*, but here the incubus is a horse ridden by a *sans-culotte*, and the print satirizes his Jacobinical sentiments [37]. Fox's political opponent, the younger William Pitt, appears in another print as the incubus, with John Bull as the victim, and a French Jacobin replacing Fuseli's horse and glowering through the window [38]. Britain, personified either as John Bull or Britannia, appears as the sleeping figure in some later prints [39]. But Napoleon and Louis XVIII were also to be shown experiencing nightmares [40, 41]. Yet

THE NIGHT MARE.

37. Caricature of C. J. Fox,
1799. By R.S.

38. Caricature of William Pitt,
1795. Temple Webb

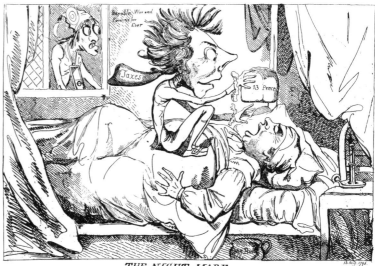

THE NIGHT MARE
Pub Aug 13 1795 by S W Fores N 50 Piccadilly the Corner of Sackville St Folio of characters lent out for the Evening

39. *John Bull's Night Mare*, 1828. R. Seymour

40. *Napoleon Dreaming in his Cell*, 1814. G. Cruikshank

41. *Louis the Fat Troubled with the Night Mare* 1823. G. Cruikshank

42. *The Nightmare or the Source of the Nile*, *c.* 1798. Anonymous

another print, of a distinctly scabrous cast, shows Emma Hamilton as the victim and Nelson as the incubus lifting her dress [42].

These various travesties reveal how potent an image Fuseli had created. It is not therefore surprising that he should have returned to the theme on only one other occasion – in a wash drawing showing

ʿαἐϑιϲαιιϵϲαν· καλοι γηϲʹοναϲ κεφαλαͻϑιν ἐπωϲτη
ϲͻϲ ϝυϲτʹ

Q.E.Hϋι
ϲϵͼ.

43. *The Nightmare*, 1810. J. H. Fuseli

44. *Mars and Venus* (detail), 1585.
H. Goltzius

the nightmare leaving the room of two sleeping girls [43]. Here he made use of another precedent in sixteenth-century art, basing his two main figures almost line for line on a print of Mars and Venus by Henrik Goltzius of which he is known to have possessed a copy [44].[74] It is a prime example of his 'judicious adoption of figures in art'. Fuseli inscribed the drawing in Greek, 'but the heavily dreaming girls are troubled by bad dreams in the night'; it is

difficult to imagine why such an innocent statement should have
been made in the decent obscurity of a learned language.

Fuseli re-used the posture of the sleeping girl in his original
Nightmare in several later works. She figures as the daughter in
Count Ugolino which he painted in 1806 in direct rivalry with
Reynolds's picture of the same subject [45]. More significantly,

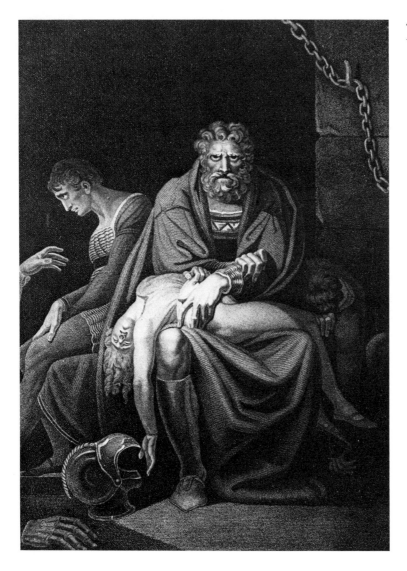

45. *Count Ugolino*, 1806.
After J. H. Fuseli

perhaps, she appears as Truth, trampled on by religious fanaticism and folly in an undated mezzotint [46]. For this print may serve to underline the rationalist background to *The Nightmare* itself, since the figure of religious fanaticism is a parody of an accepted baroque personification of Faith – as, for instance, in Théodon's marble group of *The Triumph of Faith over Paganism* in the Gesù in Rome.

46. Religious Fanaticism trampling upon Truth,
c. 1780–90. J. H. Fuseli

According to B. R. Haydon *The Nightmare* was 'decidedly popular all over Europe'.[75] Prints were transmitted very quickly from one country to another and Fuseli's composition became widely available in 1783, as soon as an engraving of it was issued.

47. *The Dream of Eleanor, c.* 1795
G. Kininger

(We have already seen that a copy was on display at the Leipzig fair in January 1783.) And before long its influence can be observed in Continental works of art. There is, for instance, the figure of the dead Cleopatra in a painting by Regnault of about 1805, and, even closer to Fuseli, a strange drawing by Georg Kininger now in the Albertina in Vienna [47]. An inscription reveals that this represents the 'Songe d'Eléonore, épouse de Richard Coeur de Lion, sujet

48. *A Nightmare, c.* 1800.
N. Abildgaard

tiré du ballet de ce nom.' A pantomime ballet entitled *Richard Löwenherz König von England* by Salvatore Vigano was indeed performed at the Kärtnertor theatre in Vienna on 2 February 1795.

A painting of a nightmare by Nicolai Abildgaard (whom Fuseli had known in Rome in the 1770s) is still more obviously derived from Fuseli [48]. Though undated, it was probably painted in the last years of the eighteenth or the first of the nineteenth century.

Here the incubus is unaccompanied by a horse and has lost all contact with the classical ancestry of Fuseli's, while the sleeping figure is still further removed from its source. This work has been called a copy after Fuseli, but it should perhaps be termed a comment on him. Abildgaard painted, in fact, a distinctly nordic version of the theme, which seems to accept, rather than to rationalize, the mystery of a nocturnal visitation.

But the work that most insistently challenges comparison with Fuseli's picture is, of course, Goya's Capricho no. 43 *El sueño de la razón produce monstruos* – the sleep of reason produces monsters [49].[76] There may even be a reminiscence of Fuseli's victim in two other Caprichos – no. 9 *Tantalo* [50], a girl in white with her arm hanging down, and no. 8 *Que se la llevaron* (they carried her off), a girl in white with her head hanging back. There is, however, more than a difference in artistic quality between *The Nightmare* and Goya's *Sleep of Reason*. Goya's own comment on his print was: 'Fantasy abandoned by reason produces impossible monsters. United with her, she is the mother of all arts and the source of their wonders.' Yet, as Michael Levey has pointed out, a genuine psychological sense of oppression is conveyed by Goya's image 'with its ceaseless beat of wings darkening the air, and with, too, its suggestion that these horrible creatures come from within the mind'.[77] He quotes Pope's question as unanswered by Fuseli:

With terrors round can reason hold her throne,
Despise the known, not tremble at the unknown?
Survey both worlds, intrepid and entire,
In spite of witches, devils, dreams and fire?

At the height of the romantic period in France, Fuseli's composition was adapted on at least three occasions by the book illustrator Tony Johannot. In a print entitled quite simply *Rêve* [51] he showed a girl lying in exactly the same posture as the victim in *The Nightmare* with a cloud of monsters hovering above her. As an illustration to *Les Intimes*, a novel by 'Michel Raymond' – des-

49 *(left)*. *The Sleep of Reason,* 1796–8. Goya

50. Capricho no. 9, 1796–8. Goya

51. *Rêve*,
c. 1830. After Tony Johannot

52. *Cauchemar*,
1830. After Tony Johannot

cribed by a reviewer of 1830 as 'un vrai cauchemar, croyez-moi!' – he drew a sleeping figure with an incubus of peculiar malevolence squatting on his or her chest [52]. And in 1845 he elaborated this composition to serve as a frontispiece for a new edition of Charles Nodier's *Smarra ou les démons de la nuit* [53]. This conte, first published in 1821, is one of the many manifestations of the cult of vampirism which enjoyed much popularity in France after the publication of *The Vampire*, a poem by Polidori, incorrectly supposed to have been written by Byron. Nodier appears to have been inspired by the writings of Alberto Fortis and Giovanni

53. *Smarra*, 1845. After Tony Johannot

Lovrich which, as we have already seen, were probably known to Fuseli. But it is clear that he was thinking of Goya rather than of Fuseli when he wrote, 'as soon as my eye-lids, weary of struggling against dreaded sleep, close from oppression, the monsters appear... They circle around me, making me giddy with their cries, frightening me with their frolics, and fouling my trembling lips with their harpy caresses.'[78]

In England, over-familiarity with Fuseli's nightmare image[79] through caricatures and prints led to its devaluation in the later nineteenth century – to such popular travesties as the lithograph of *The Racing Nightmare*, after a painting by A. C. Havell, published in 1891 [54].

54. *The Racing Nightmare* (detail), 1891. After A. C. Havell

On 16 April 1825 B. R. Haydon wrote in his journal: 'Fuzeli is dead and [in] my opinion is an irreparable loss . . . Notwithstanding the apathy of the public latterly towards his work. Fuzeli has had his day.'[80] By this date, indeed, his works must have seemed sadly old fashioned. Chroniclers of English painting paid lip-service to him throughout the nineteenth century, generally commenting that Michelangelo had proved to be his evil genius. It was not until the 1920s that serious attention was directed to his life and works. The moment is significant for his rediscovery coincides with the revival of interest in the Mannerists – to whom he had been so frequently indebted, though this was not pointed out in the 1930s – and with the Surrealist movement. By critics, if not by artists, Fuseli was soon hailed as a precursor of Surrealism. Ruthven Todd in England and Edmond Jaloux in France both presented him in this way.[81] And as late as 1950 an art critic of *The Times*, in a singularly obtuse notice, remarked that 'he is not to be taken seriously as an artist and there could hardly be a sillier movement of taste than that which has made him increasingly fashionable ever since he was first elected a surrealist under rule 2'.

The Surrealist movement may partly account for the revival of interest in Fuseli. But that is not to suggest that he was in any meaningful sense a precursor of it. Surrealism was defined by André Breton as 'Pure psychic automatism, by which it is intended to express verbally, in writing or in any other way, the true process of thought, free from the exercise of reason, and every aesthetic or moral preoccupation'. The subtlest casuist could hardly reconcile that statement of intention with *The Nightmare*. To regard this picture as a precocious example of nineteenth-century Romanticism, let alone of Surrealism, is to misunderstand it.

Nor can the picture be interpreted in terms of Freudian dream analysis. As I remarked at the beginning of this study, Freud possessed a print of *The Nightmare* but never referred to it in his published works. Nor did Fuseli's compatriot, Jung, show any more interest. A photograph of it was reproduced in a posthumously published collection of his writings, but he never referred to it in print either in this book or elsewhere. Both Freud and Jung were concerned primarily with the subconscious minds of individuals. For them Fuseli's painting may well have seemed too generalized to be of interest – a painting about nightmares rather than a visualization of the subconscious fantasy of a particular person, of a specific case. For Fuseli had not set out to illustrate a dream so much as to depict the sensation of terror and stifling oppression experienced in a nightmare.

Fuseli rendered a subconscious phenomenon in terms agreeable to his own intellectual outlook. But we must beware of falling into what has been called the heresy of 'intentionalism'. If *The Night-mare* were no more than a 'gothic horror' picture and a collection of late eighteenth-century theories about nightmares expressed in visual forms filched – or as he would have said 'judiciously adopted' – from the art of past epochs, it would hardly hold much appeal for us today. Yet it does retain an extraordinary power – a power conspicuously lacking in such other dream pictures as Moritz von Schwind's *Traum des Gefangenen* which Freud analysed, or, indeed in most of Fuseli's other canvases: the illustrations to Milton for instance, by which he hoped and expected to achieve immortality.

The Nightmare continues to hold the modern observer partly because it is generalized, partly because it represents an everyday – or everynight – phenomenon in terms which are instantly comprehensible. For he made a raid on what Jung was to call the 'collective unconscious'. Though his own outlook was rational, he drew on a stock of legends and beliefs which survived and still survive at the back of the European mind. In this picture he fused ancient stories – old wives' tales and folk legends – and odd lines of poetry about the devil, witches, incubi and succubi, magic steeds, love and desire and hate into one unforgettable image. It is an image which retains its force despite all that has been discovered about the workings of the unconscious mind since 1782.

Appendix I:
Versions and Variants

1. *The Preliminary Sketch.* In his biography of Fuseli, Knowles tells us that he then owned the original study for *The Nightmare*, inscribed *St Martin's Lane, March 1781*, and that in this work the horse had not yet put in an appearance.[82] The work to which he refers was presumably lot 7 'The Nightmare, a vision' which Knowles bought for sixteen guineas in the sale of Fuseli's paintings and drawings at Christie's, 28 May 1827. Scholars from Ganz to Janson have assumed that this is identical with the chalk drawing, 48 x 69 cm. [21], presented in March 1885 from the Julia Carrick-Moore collection to the British Museum. (Dr James Carrick-Moore was a friend of the Locks of Norbury whom Fuseli met after his return from Rome.) The drawing has right-handed shading throughout and I have never accepted it because I do not believe that Fuseli executed any right-handed work after his illness in Venice in 1772. Schiff accepts it with reservations, as his no. 841, 'on the upper surface there are hatchings by a right-handed draughtsman, but which could have been added after fading in the original drawing . . . the execution seems strong enough to be a work from Fuseli's hand'.[83] The Carrick-Moore drawing differs from all the other versions not only in the omission of the horse but also in the absence of a scent bottle from the table. It is in black chalk heightened with white – a very unusual medium for Fuseli. In spite of the missing horse, I would accept this drawing, at the most, as a copy after a lost original sketch for the first version of the painting. On the other hand, it may have been worked on in preparation for an engraving but not, of course, by Fuseli himself. Janson has pointed out that the alignment of the legs and toes

derives from the figure of a male corpse lying on his back in the centre of the Noah panel on Ghiberti's Baptistery doors in Florence – but this particular feature recurs in none of Fuseli's painted versions of *The Nightmare*.

2. *The First Version* [Colour Plate]. The painting in the Detroit Institute of Arts 101 x 124.5 cm., bought in London in 1955 from the Haskett-Smith collection, was first identified as the picture which Fuseli exhibited at the Royal Academy in London in 1782, by H. W. Janson. Part of the evidence for this identification is provided by engravings which repeat the composition of the Detroit picture. The first, in colour and aquatint by Laurede, is dated 1782 and was presumably pirated. The authorized version, for which Fuseli was paid twenty guineas, was engraved by T. Burke and published by J. R. Smith on 30 January 1783. Burke engraved and Smith published a series of prints after Fuseli from this date until 1802. There is also by them a colour and aquatint print of *The Nightmare* dated 1802. A colour aquatint was also produced by de Ville Neuve in 1784.

3. *Frankfurt Version*. This version [7], the one most frequently reproduced in recent literature, 77 x 64 cm., was acquired by the Goethe Museum, Frankfurt-am-Main, from the Ganz collection. This work differs from the Detroit version in that it is upright; the horse is white; the incubus is more cat-like and smiles while playing a pipe; the table is behind and not in front of the bed; the girl lies with her head to the left and her arm hanging down towards the outer edge of the canvas; she lies on a bolster, as if to ease impregnation; and her knees are raised. It seems more than probable that Fuseli executed this painting as a specially requested commission, inspired by the popularity of the original version. For it was Fuseli's usual habit to repeat almost line for line, except when working in upright format as in the series of illustrations for the Rivington Shakespeare of 1805. Stylistically the Frankfurt version is not so very different from that in Detroit and one may assume that it was painted soon after 1782: Janson dates it about 1785 to 1790,

Schiff more firmly 1790–91. I feel that the painting should be dated more cautiously, between 1782 and 1791. Janson has suggested that this version may owe something to Jacques Blanchard's *Death of Cleopatra* (*c*.1630) at Chatsworth but also known by engravings.

4. *Version in Collection of Frau Marg-Socin, Basle*. This painting, 75 x 95 cm., bought from the Earl of Harrowby, formerly in the collections of Stafford and the Countess of Guilford, is a late variant of the Detroit version. The horse is darkish; the girl is formalized; the incubus has the pose of that in the Detroit version but the cat-like features of the Frankfurt version. One new feature is introduced: on the table there is a statuette group of a man and a girl.

5. *The Countess of Guilford's Picture* [55]. The engraved inscription on a print by W. Raddon, dated 19 April 1827, states that it was after a picture in the collection of the Countess of Guilford.[84] Unless we are to assume engraver's licence – by no means unlikely – this print records a lost version. The incubus looks over his right

55. *The Nightmare*, 1827. W. Raddon after J. H. Fuseli

shoulder, as in the Detroit version, the horse is nearly central as in no. 4, and the table supports a miniature group as in number 4, but here they are both female, a comb, three pins and a pair of ear-rings. A somewhat angry-looking owl sits on the windowsill.

6. *Vassar version.* A small painting, 32.4 x 23 cm., which was acquired by the Vassar College Art Collection, in 1966. The format is upright, but in almost all other respects this repeats the composition of the Detroit version.[85]

Appendix II:
Check-list of Caricatures
and Satirical Prints

I am deeply indebted to the late Mrs Dorothy George for information about the following prints (except no. 4); see also her *English Political Caricature*, vol. I, to 1792, and vol. II, 1793–1832, London, 1959.

1. *The Covent Garden Nightmare* by T. Rowlandson, 1784 (British Museum 6543). Issued at the time of the Westminster election; Charles James Fox dreams of defeat. The toilet articles in Fuseli's painting are replaced by dice and dice-box. This appears to be the first English political caricature based on the travesty of a painting [3].

    2. *A Night Mare* by R. Newton, 26 October 1794 (British Museum 8555). A burlesque of the painting without political significance [4].

    3. *The Night Mare*, anonymous, dated 13 August 1795 (British Museum 8671), showing John Bull in bed, William Pitt as the incubus and a French Jacobin looking through the window in the place of Fuseli's horse. Possibly by Temple Webb [38].

    4. *The Night Mare*, anonymous *c.* 1798, inscribed in the place usually occupied by the name of the publisher, 'NB the greatest rarity in Europe constantly on sale'. The book on the chair *Travels &c* is probably James Bruce: *Travels to Discover the Source of the Nile* (London, 1790) and the chamber-pot is inscribed, *the Source of the Nile*. The print seems to represent Nelson and Lady Hamilton; it was probably issued after the battle of the Nile in 1798. (Not in British Museum) [42].

5. *The Night Mare*, by R. S. (unidentified), 1 May 1799 (British Museum 9371). Published in the *Anti-Jacobin Review*, 1 May 1799, as an illustration to verses attacking Charles James Fox who is shown with a horse on his chest ridden by a sans-culotte and Napoleon wrenching at his out-thrown head [37].

6. *The Singular Dream of a Girl at York*, anonymous, 1802 (British Museum 9946). A close copy of Fuseli's composition but crude and ill-drawn. It is perhaps from a chap-book and is clearly non-political.

7. *The Dutch Night-Mare or the Fraternal Hug returned with a Dutch Squeeze*, by T. Rowlandson, 29 November 1813 (British Museum 12105). Napoleon is shown in bed with a Dutchman on his chest blowing tobacco smoke at him: an allusion to the liberation of Holland. A close copy, presumably Dutch, is recorded (M. D. George op. cit., p. 150).

8. *Napoleon Dreaming in his Cell at the Military College*, by George Cruikshank, 10 November 1814 (British Museum 12455). Aquatint illustration to Doctor Syntax (William Combe): *The Life of Napoleon*, London, 1815, showing the young Napoleon (*c.* 1794) dreaming with a phantom ass or mule ridden by a demon on his chest and various symbols of his career in the background [40].

9. *The Night Mayor Painted by Fuzely*, anonymous print, 1816, (British Museum 12817). A satire on Matthew Wood, Lord Mayor of London, who initiated a campaign against prostitutes in the City. He is shown in his mayoral gown, squatting on a large and apparently drunken prostitute; Fuseli's horse is replaced by Silvester, the City Recorder, notorious for his harsh and reactionary views on crime and punishment [5].

10. *Louis the Fat Troubled with the Night Mare and Dreams of Terror*, by George Cruikshank, May 1823 (British Museum 14521). No more than a distant echo of Fuseli. Louis XVIII is shown in bed, with Mme de Cayle awake beside him; Napoleon and his son, the head of Louis XVI, and Spanish troops putting the French to flight form the subjects of his nightmare [41].

11. *John Bull's Night Mare*, by R. Seymour, *c.* January 1828 (British Museum 15497). A satire on Henry Hunt's proposals for radical reform; John Bull is shown in bed, ill and miserable, with the incubus labelled 'National Debt' on his chest [39].

12. *Figaro's Prophetic*, by R. Seymour, 20 June 1832 (British Museum 17162/2). Britannia is shown as the victim of the nightmare. Copied from Moore's Almanack.

13. *The Birmingham Night Mare*, by R. Seymour, 1 July 1832 (British Museum 17177). A satire on Thomas Attwood, founder of the Birmingham Political Union (23 January 1830), who is shown as the incubus squatting on the breast of Britannia [6].

Notes

The following abbreviations are used in the notes:

Antal: Frederick Antal: *Fuseli Studies* (London, 1956)

Cunningham: Allan Cunningham: *The Lives of the Most Eminent British Painters*, 1829, ed. Mrs Charles Heaton (London, 1879)

Janson: H. W. Janson: 'Fuseli's *Nightmare*' in *Arts and Sciences*, Spring 1963, pp. 23–8

Jones: Ernest Jones: *On the Nightmare* (London, 1931)

Knowles: John Knowles: *The Life and Writings of Henry Fuseli M.A., R.A.* (London, 1831)

Powell: Nicolas Powell: *The Drawings of Henry Fuseli* (London, 1951)

Schiff: G. Schiff: *Johann Heinrich Füssli* (1741–1825), Zurich and Munich, 1972.

1. Max Eastman: *Heroes I Have Known*, New York, 1942, p. 264. I am indebted for this reference to Professor Jack Spector who tells me that he visited Freud's apartment in Vienna in 1969 but did not see the print displayed. Mrs Anna Freud told him that she had never seen such a print but that information about it might be obtained from Ernst Freud (the psychologist's brother) who died soon afterwards.

2. Jones: *On the Nightmare*, London, 1931.

3. S. Freud: *Introductory Lectures on Psycho-Analysis* (tr. James Strachey, standard ed., vol. XV, London, 1963, p. 135). Schwind also painted a *Dream of Adam c.* 1824 (O. Weighmann: *Schwind*, Klassiker der Kunst, vol. IX, Stuttgart, 1906, p. 26). Freud's own dream of a swimming pool incorporated images from Schwind's *Legend of Mélusine* (*On Dreams*, standard edition, vol. V, London, 1953, p. 649).

4. *The Romantic Era* (exhibition catalogue), Herron Museum of Art, Indianapolis, 1965, no. 22.

5. K. Wagner, ed.: *Briefe an und von Merck*, Darmstadt, 1838, p. 389.

6. Commenting on the song of Edgar in *King Lear*, Coleridge (writing to Southey in December 1794) misquoted the passage:

St Withold footed thrice the Oulds,
He met the nightmare and her nine foals;
He bade her alight and her troth plight,
And, "Aroynt thee, Witch!" he said.

'Would not this be a subject for a wild ode? . . . I shall set about one when I am in a humour to abandon myself to all the diableries that ever met the eye of a Fuseli.'

7. 'The Late Mr. Fuseli' in *New Monthly Magazine,* May 1831, p. 435.

8. For both Winckelmann and Goethe, opposition to the rococo in art was closely associated with opposition to France.

9. Goethe has little to say about Fuseli, but his artistic mentor J. H. Meyer wrote of him, *Entwurf einer Kunstgeschichte des achtzehnten Jahrhunderts,* Tübingen, 1805: 'Von den neueren Bekennern des Michelangelo hat keiner mehr Talent gezeigt noch grösseren Ruhm erworben als Heinrich Füessli . . . Nicht nur trachtete er die gewaltigen Formen seines Vorbildes nachzuahmen, sondern fügte noch düstere Beleuchtung und Grausen erregende Gegenstände hinzu, um, wäre es ihm möglich gewesen, das Entsetzliche hervorzubringen. Seine Darstellungen waren daher meistens Hexen und Gespenster nach Volkssagen, erschütternde Szenen aus Shakespeare und anderen tragischen Dichtern' (in J. W. Goethe: *Winckelmann und sein Jahrhundert,* ed. Helmut Holtzhauer, Leipzig, 1969, p. 168). *The Nightmare* is the only one of Fuseli's paintings drawn from folk-lore.

10. J. C. Füssli's main publications were, *Geschichte und Abbildung d. besten Maler in d. Schweiz,* 2 vols. Zurich, 1755-7; *Leben der berühmten Maler Rugendas und Kupetzky,* Zurich, 1758; *Raisonnier. Verzeichnis der vornehmsten Kupferstecher und ihrer Werke,* 1771. He was responsible for publishing A. R. Mengs, *Gedanken über die Schönheit,* 1765 and an account of Winckelmann's letters to his friends in Switzerland, as a postscript to L. Usteri's edition of Winckelmann's correspondence (1778).

11. The relationships between various members of the Füssli family were established in Thieme-Becker *Künstler-Lexikon,* vol. xii, pp. 565-73. Johann Rudolf, the son of Johann Caspar, has, none the less, often been confused with his cousin.

12. Antal, p. 9; I have drawn on this source extensively for information about Fuseli's early years.

13. This is the account generally given. One may, however, ask if Johann Caspar did not notice in his son intellectual qualities which encouraged him to believe that the boy would benefit from a better education than that deemed necessary for an artist. In the social hierarchy of the times a pastor ranked above a painter.

14. He is said to have been ambidextrous until 1772 when he was seriously ill in Venice: after that date he appears to have drawn only with his left hand.

15. G. H. Lewes, *The Life and Works of Goethe*, London, 1855, vol. i, p. 273. The standard biography of Lavater is C. Jannetzky, *Johann Caspar Lavater*, Frauenfeld, 1928.

16. For Fuseli and *Sturm und Drang* friendship, see K. Lankheit, *Das Freundschaftsbild der Romantik*, Heidelberg, 1952, pp. 74–81. For Fuseli's letters to Lavater, see Eudo C. Mason, *The Mind of Henry Fuseli*, London, 1951, pp. 96–103.

17. While he and Lavater were staying in Spalding's cottage at Barth in Pomerania, Fuseli painted the walls of a summer house with illustrations to Spalding's works: *Virtue and Religion hand in hand, point out Immortality to Man*, and *Time Cutting the Wings of Desire*.

18. P. Gay, *The Enlightenment, An Interpretation: The Rise of Modern Paganism*, New York, 1966, p. 330.

19. James Boswell met Andrew (later Sir Andrew) Mitchell in Berlin in 1764 and referred to him frequently in his journal, see F. A. Pottle, ed., *Boswell on the Grand Tour: Germany and Switzerland 1764*, London, 1953, pp. 20–91.

20. Fuseli was later to change his attitude to Winckelmann and wrote in the introduction to his *Lectures*: 'Winckelmann was the parasite of the fragments that fell from the conversation of the tablets of Mengs, a deep scholar, and better fitted to comment a classic than to give lessons on art and style: he reasoned himself into frigid reveries and Platonic dreams on beauty . . . To him Germany owes the shackles of her artists, and the narrow limits of her aim; from him they have learned to substitute the means for the end, and, by a hopeless chase after what they call beauty, to lose what alone can make beauty interesting – expression and mind.' Knowles, vol. ii, p. 13.

21. Reynolds wrote to Barry: 'Whoever has great views, I would recommend to him, whilst at Rome, rather to live on bread and water than to lose advantages which he can never hope to enjoy a second time,

and which he will find only in the Vatican; where, I will engage, no cavalier sends his students to copy for him. The Capella Sistina is the production of the greatest genius that was ever employed in the arts; it is worth considering by what principles that stupendous greatness of style is produced; and endeavouring to produce something of your own on those principles, will be a more advantageous method of studying than copying the St Cecilia in the Borghese, or the Herodias of Guido, which may be copied to eternity without contributing a jot towards making a man a more able painter. If you neglect visiting the Vatican often, and particularly the Capella Sistina, you will neglect receiving that peculiar advantage which Rome can give above all other cities in the world. In other places you will find casts from the antique, and capital pictures of the great painters; but it is there only that you can see the works of Michael Angelo and Raphael.' Cunningham, vol. i, p. 211-12. The *St Cecilia* in the Borghese to which Reynolds refers is a painting by Domenichino still in Villa Borghese but now identified as a *Sybil*: the *Herodias* is probably Guido Reni's *Salome*, then in Palazzo Corsini, now in the Galleria Nazionale, Rome. For other attitudes to Michelangelo in eighteenth-century England see G. Melchiori: *Michelangelo nel Settecento Inglese*, Rome, 1950.

22. For Fuseli in the Sistine Chapel, Cunningham, vol. ii, p. 48. The quotation from Winckelmann is from Fuseli's own translation, *Reflections on the Painting and Sculpture of the Greeks*, London, 1765.

23. In the British Museum, London, and the Kunsthaus, Zurich, cf. Powell, p. 37 and pl. 10.

24. For Fuseli's comments on the representation of the death of Germanicus, see his third lecture, Knowles, vol. ii, p. 177-8. The relief by Thomas Banks is at Holkham Hall, Norfolk, cf. C. F. Bell: *Annals of Thomas Banks*, Cambridge, 1938, pp. 35-43, pl. ii.

25. Painted in 1761 but now known only from the engraving by T. Cunego, 1765. For Gavin Hamilton's influence at this time see E. K. Waterhouse in *Proceedings of the British Academy*, 1954, pp. 57-74.

26. C. F. Bell, op. cit., p. 16.

27. Byron wrote in his journal, 20 March 1814: 'There is a fine engraving in Lavater, from a picture by Fuseli, of *that* Ezzelin, over the body of Meduna, punished by him for a *hitch* in her constancy during his absence in the Crusades. He was right - but I want to know the story.' (P. Quennell: *Byron: A Self-Portrait*, London, 1950, p. 254.) The conversation is recorded by Knowles, vol. i, p. 403.

28. A. M. Stirling, *The Richmond Papers*, London, 1926.

29. E. Young: *Conjectures on Original Composition*, London, 1759.

30. Fuseli owned prints by Marcantonio Raimondi. He is also known to have possessed an example of Agostino Veneziano's engraving after Giulo Romano *Il Stregozzo* which he described in his *Aphorisms* as 'an association of ideas big with the very elements of dreams', Knowles, vol. iii, p. 145. For Ghisi's *Dream of Raphael* see: *Graphische Sammlung Albertina: Die Kunst der Graphik II*[6]: *Renaissance in Italien 16 Jahrhundert*, Vienna 1966, no. 309.

31. G. Levitine in *Art Bulletin* XXXVII (1955), p. 56. Many comments on monsters in art seem to have been inspired by a passage in Vitruvius, Book VII, chap. 5.

32. Knowles, vol. ii, pp. 102-3.

33. R. Burton, *Anatomy of Melancholy*, 1621, Pt. 2, sec. 2, memo. 5, declares: 'Against fearful and troublesome dreams, *incubus*, and such inconvenience, wherewith melancholy men are molested, the best remedy is to eat a light supper, and of such meats as are easy of digestion, no hare, venison, beef etc.'

34. Cunningham, vol. ii, p. 93.

35. T. Hobbes, *Leviathan*, London, 1651, pt. 1, chap. 2, p. 6.

36. ibid, chap. 12, p. 53.

37. J. Locke, *Essay Concerning Human Understanding*, London, 1690, in *Works*, 1714, vol. i, p. 36.

38. ibid, p. 37.

39. Letter to S. Dälliker cited by E. Gradmann and A. M. Cetto, *Schweizer Malerei im 17 und 18 Jahrhundert*, Basle, 1944, p. 74.

40. I Kant, *Anthropologie*, 1798, Sec. 34, p. 105.

41. P. Stern, *Lichtenberg: A Doctrine of Scattered Occasions*, London, 1963, pp. 70-71, 230-32.

42. Quoted by O. Walzel, *German Romanticism*, New York, 1932, p. 245. For a general account of romantic attitudes to dreams see Albert Béguin, *L'âme romantique et le rêve*, Paris, 1939.

43. Quoted by Jones, p. 45.

44. R. Burton, op. cit. Pt. 1, sec. 3, memb. 2, subs. 4.

45. T. Hobbes, op. cit. p. 55.

46. R. Burton, op. cit. Pt. 3, sec. 2, memb. 1, subs. 2. Elsewhere, however, Burton takes a more rational line, cf. note 33 above and pt. 1, sec. 2, memb. 3, subs. 2: 'sleepers, which by reason of humours and concourse of vapours troubling the phantasy, imagine many times

absurd and prodigious things, and in such as are troubled with *incubus*, or witch ridden (as we call it); if they lie on their backs, they suppose an old woman rides and sits so hard upon them that they are almost stifled for want of breath; when there is nothing that offends but a concourse of bad humours, which trouble the phantasy.'

47. H. R. Trevor-Roper, *The European Witch Craze of the 16th and 17th Centuries*, Harmondsworth, 1969.

48. C. G. Jung, *Psychology of the Unconscious*, London, 1944, p. 170, for other remarks on nightmares, p. 154. For an account of the deep rooted subconscious beliefs of countrymen about horses etc. see G. E. Evans, *The Pattern Under the Plough*, London, 1966.

49. Janson, p. 24.

50. Janson, p. 28. See also E. P. Richardson in *Bulletin of the Detroit Institute of Arts*, xxxiv, 1954–5, pp. 2–3.

51. Kunsthaus, Zurich.

52. In his *Aphorisms* nos. 224 and 216, Knowles, vol. ii, p. 143 and 141.

53. *Aphorism* 223, Knowles, ibid, p. 143.

54. Knowles, ibid, p. 297. The passage also recalls Burton (who often cites Paracelsus): 'it troubles me to think of, much more to relate, those frequent aborts and murderings of infants in their nunneries (read Kemnisius and others), their notorious fornications, those *spintrias*, *tribadas*, *ambubaias* etc., those rapes, incests, adulteries, masturpations, sodomies, buggeries of monks and friars' (op. cit. pt. I, sec. 3, memb. 2, subs. 4).

55. Knowles, ibid, p. 144.

56. B. R. Haydon, op. cit. vol. i, p. 232. The passage was written in 1815 but is a re-working of a diary entry made on 27 April 1812: 'Think of Fuzeli's savage ferocity, his whorish abandoned women, the daughters of the bawds of Hell, engendered by lecherous, dusky demons . . . Again think of Fuzeli's men, the sons of banditti, and contrast them with the rapturous innocence of St John [by Raphael] . . .'

57. Mary Wollstonecraft's passion for Fuseli was fully described by her widower, William Godwin: *Memoirs of the Author of A Vindication of the Rights of Women*, London, 1798.

58. Leigh Hunt, *Autobiography*, revised ed. London, 1860, pp. 188–9.

59. E. J. Morley (ed.): *Henry Crabb Robinson on Books and their Writers*, London, 1938, p. 34: 'June 6th [1811] . . . At the exhibition where I found but little to gratify me. Coleridge there: he pointed out to

me the 'vigorous impotence' of Fuseli, whose *Macbeth* is, indeed, a very disgusting production.'

60. Knowles, ibid, p. 180.

61. Knowles, vol. i, p. 386.

62. Reynolds's debt to this painting was first noted by E. Wind, *Journal of the Warburg Institute* II (1938), p. 183.

63. Antal, p. 92, first suggested *Hecuba's Dream* as a source for *The Nightmare*.

64. Janson, p. 27.

65. Antal, p. 93. For Fuseli's copy see Powell, pl. 12.

66. Professor Janson has kindly told me that after the publication of his article, Professor Meyer Schapiro suggested this to him.

67. Several antique (or supposedly antique) statues of Silenus in a crouching posture were known in the eighteenth century. The engraving reproduced in [33] is taken from F. de Clarac: *Musée de Sculpture*, Paris, 1841–50 where it is described (vol. iii, p. 277) as being 'à Cambridge' though no such figure was known to Michaelis or is now in any Cambridge collection. The Clarac engraving is probably derived from a late-eighteenth-century drawing or print. For the bronze 'hunch-backed beggar' see G. Becatti: *The Art of Ancient Greece and Rome*, London, 1968, pl. 258.

68. These pieces are not very close to any known examples of English furniture dating from the 1770s or 1780s but, Dr Kreisel informs me, they have similarities with German furniture of this period.

69. Quoted by A. Graves: *The Royal Academy ... A Complete Dictionary*, London, 1905–6.

70. See Norman D. Ziff in *Burlington Magazine*, CXII (1970), pp. 531–5.

71. For a general account of the sublime see S. H. Monk: *The Sublime*, 1935 (revised edn. Ann Arbor, 1960). It is perhaps worth recording Burke's remarks on horses: 'The horse in the light of a useful beast, fit for the plough, the road, the draft; in every social, useful light, the horse has nothing sublime: but is it thus that we are affected with him, *whose neck is clothed with thunder, the glory of whose nostrils is terrible, who swalloweth the ground with fierceness and rage, neither believeth that it is the sound of the trumpet?* In this description, the useful character of the horse entirely disappears, and the terrible and sublime burst out together.' E. Burke: *A Philosophical Inquiry into the Origins of our Ideas on the Sublime and Beautiful*, London, 1757, Pt. ii, sec. 5.

72. Knowles, vol. ii, p. 156.

73. F. Cummings in *Romantic Art in Britain* (exhibition catalogue), Detroit Institute of Arts and Philadelphia Museum of Art, 1968, p. 125.

74. First noted by Antal, p. 102: Fuseli repeated certain elements of *The Nightmare* in his painting of *Belinda's Dream* (illustrating a passage in Pope's *The Rape of the Lock*) now in the Vancouver Art Gallery. Unfortunately the article in which this work was first published, Harold D. Kalman: 'Füssli, Pope and the Nightmare', in *Pantheon* XXIX (1971) pp. 226–36, appeared after the present book went to press and I was therefore unable to make use of it. Dr Kalman draws attention to the toilet articles which appear in both *The Nightmare* and the Vancouver picture – the jars and looking-glass (in which Dr Kalman perceives a crack) – identifying them as emblems of the fragility of feminine chastity. He suggests that *The Nightmare* is an illustration to the Queen Mab speech in *Romeo and Juliet*. This seems forced to me. Fuseli certainly painted original subjects, see p. 34. If *The Nightmare* was intended as an illustration to the Queen Mab speech it is very extraordinary that no one should have remarked on this at the time. That the Queen Mab speech, as well as many other things, was at the back of Fuseli's mind when he conceived the painting is certainly possible as, indeed, I suggest on p. 53

75. B. R. Haydon, op. cit. vol. iii, p. 14.

76. F. D. Klingender, *Hogarth and English Caricature*, London, 1945, p. 16.

77. Michael Levey, *Rococo to Revolution*, London, 1966, pp. 10–12.

78. Charles Nodier, *Contes*, Paris, 1961, p. 65: the relationship of the passage quoted to the Goya is pointed out by the editor of this edition, Pierre-Georges Castex. Tony Johannot's print [53] was reproduced in *L'Artiste*, series i, vol. i (1830–31) p. 170. A few years later it reappeared in the Spanish Magazine *El Artista* III (1836) p. 72, where it was entitled 'La Pesadilla' and ascribed to Federico Madrazo y Kuntz without acknowledgement to Johannot.

79. Coleridge is responsible for the most notable nightmare image in English romantic poetry – the lines he inserted in the 1817 version of the *Rime of the Ancient Mariner*,

> *The Night-mare LIFE-IN-DEATH was she,*
> *Who thicks man's blood with cold.*

As we have already seen, he was aware of Fuseli's work and it is possible that the horse in Fuseli's *Nightmare* led him to misquote Shakespeare's 'nightmare and her nine fold' as 'nightmare and her nine foals' (cf. note 6). But he was not a great admirer of Fuseli whom he described as a 'brusher up of Convulsia and Tetanus upon innocent canvas'. His remarks on nightmares in *A Course of Lectures* (*Complete Works* ed. W. G. T. Shedd, New York, 1884, vol. iv, p. 319) are however of some interest.

'It is a general, but, as it appears to me, a mistaken opinion, that in our ordinary dreams we judge the objects to be real. I say our ordinary dreams – because as to the night-mair the opinion is to a considerable extent just. But the nightmair is not a mere dream, but takes place when the waking state of the brain is recommencing and most often during a rapid alternation, a twinkling, as it were, of sleeping and waking – which either from pressure on, or some derangement in, the stomach or other digestive organs acting on the external skin (which is still in sympathy with the stomach and bowels), and benumning it, the sensations sent up to the brain by double touch (that is, when my hand touches my side or breast), are so faint as to be merely equivalent to the sensation given by a single touch, as when another person's hand touches me. The mind, therefore, which at all times, with and without distinct consciousness, seeks for and assumes, some outward cause for every impression from without, and which in sleep, by aid of the imaginative faculty, converts its judgement respecting the cause into a personal image as being the cause – the mind, I say, in this case, deceived by past experience, attributes the painful sensation received to a corresponding agent an assassin, for instance, stabbing at the side, or a goblin sitting on the breast.'

Coleridge was, of course, a sufferer from nightmares. 'The night is my Hell, Sleep my tormenting agent,' he told Tom Wedgwood in 1803. 'Three nights out of four I fall asleep, struggling to lie awake – and my frequent Night-screams have almost made me a nuisance in my own House. Dreams with me are no Shadows, but the very Substances and foot-thick Calamities of my Life'. And in *Remorse* he vividly described this 'sleep of horrors' – so different from Fuseli's *Nightmare*:

> *Now run down and stared at*
> *By forms so hideous that they mock remembrance –*
> *Now seeing nothing and imagining nothing*
> *But only being afraid – stifled with fear!*
> *While every goodly or familiar form*
> *Had a strange power of breathing terror round me!*

80. B. R. Haydon: op. cit. vol. iii, p. 14.

81. Edmond Jaloux: *Johann-Heinrich Fussli*, Geneva, 1942, p. 89, numbered him with Dali, Chirico and Max Ernst among the great surrealists and complained of his omission from an exhibition devoted to the dream held in Paris in 1939.

82. Knowles, I, 64–5, 413.

83. Schiff, no. 841.

84. Schiff, no. 1503.

85. Schiff, addenda.

List of Illustrations

Frontispiece and colour plate: *The Nightmare*. By John Henry Fuseli, 1781. Oil on canvas, 101 x 124.5 cm. Detroit, Institute of Arts, Gift of Mr and Mrs Bert L. Smokler and Mr and Mrs Lawrence A. Fleischman. (Photos: Museum.)

1. *The Nightmare*. Engraving by T. Burke after J. H. Fuseli, 1783. London, British Museum. (Photo: Museum.)

2. *Traum des Gefangenen*. By Moritz von Schwind, 1836. Oil on canvas. Munich, Schack-Galerie. (Photo: Museum.)

3. *The Covent Garden Night Mare*. Engraving by T. Rowlandson, 1784. London, British Museum. (Photo: Museum.)

4. *A Night Mare*. Etching by R. Newton, 1794. London, British Museum. (Photo: Museum.)

5. *A Night Mayor*. Anonymous print, 1816. London, British Museum. (Photo: Museum.)

6. *The Birmingham Night Mare*. Lithograph by R. Seymour, 1832. London, British Museum. (Photo: Museum.)

7. *The Nightmare*. By John Henry Fuseli. 1782-91. Oil on canvas, 75.5 x 64 cm. Frankfurt, Goethe Museum. (Photo: Museum.)

8. *The Shepherd's Dream from 'Paradise Lost'*. By J. H. Fuseli, *c.* 1798 London, Tate Gallery. (Photo: Museum.)

9. *A Satire of Marriage*. By J. H. Fuseli, *c.* 1752-60: a copy of a print in C. and R. Meyer's *Narrenbuch*. Zurich, Kunsthaus. (Photo: Museum.)

10. *The Death of Cardinal Beaufort*. By J. H. Fuseli, 1772. Pen, ink and sepia wash, sgd. *Roma '72 Fuseli*. Liverpool, Walker Art Gallery. (Photo: Museum.)

11. *Portrait of Fuseli*. By James Northcote, 1778. Oil on canvas, signed and dated. Present whereabouts unknown.

12. *Self-Portrait conversing with Johann Jakob Bodmer*. By J. H. Fuseli, 1778. Oil on canvas. Zurich, Kunsthaus. (Photo: Museum.)

13. *Ezzelin Bracciaferro Musing over Meduna, slain by him for disloyalty during his Absence*. By J. H. Fuseli, 1779. Red chalk with pen and sepia wash: dated *Zurico febr. 79*. London, British Museum. (Photo: Fine Art Engravers Ltd.)

14. *Jacob's Dream.* By Lodovico Carracci, *c.* 1605–8. Oil on canvas. Bologna, Pinacoteca. (Photo:Villani.)

15. *Hecuba's Dream.* By Giulio Romano, 1538–9. Fresco. Mantua, Palazzo Ducale. (Photo: Alinari.)

16. *Richard III visited by Ghosts.* By J. H. Fuseli, 1777. Pen, ink and grey wash: sgd. *Fusely Rome 1777.* London, British Museum. (Photo: Fine Art Engravers Ltd.)

17. *Garrick as Richard III.* By William Hogarth, *c.* 1746. Oil on canvas. Liverpool, Walker Art Gallery. (Photo: Museum.)

18. *The Dream of Raphael.* Engraving by Marcantonio Raimondi, *c.* 1506–10. London, British Museum. (Photo: Museum.)

19. *The Bewitched Groom.* Woodcut by Hans Baldung Grien, 1544. London, British Museum. (Photo: Museum.)

20. *Scene from The Tempest.* Engraving by Bromley after J. H. Fuseli, 1803.

21. *The Nightmare.* Anonymous drawing after J. H. Fuseli. London, British Museum. (Photo: Fine Art Engravers Ltd.)

22. *Portrait of a Lady.* By J. H. Fuseli, *c.* 1779, on the back of *The Nightmare* (see Frontispiece).

23. *Brunhilde and Gunther.* By J. H. Fuseli, May 1807. Nottingham, City Art Gallery. (Photo: Museum.)

24. *Lady Seated at her Dressing Table.* By J. H. Fuseli, *c.* 1780. Pencil and watercolour. Formerly London, Messrs. Tooth & Sons.

25. *The Death of Dido.* By Sir Joshua Reynolds, 1781. Oil on canvas. Reproduced by gracious permission of H.M. the Queen.

26. *Sleeping Psyche.* By Giulio Romano, 1528. Mantua, Palazzo del Tè. (Photo: Kunsthistorisches Institut, Florence.)

27. *Ariadne.* Rome, Vatican Museum. (Photo: Alinari.)

28. Detail from the Frontispiece.

29. *Venus and Mars.* By Paolo Veronese, 1575–84. Turin, Galleria Sabauda. (Photo: Alinari.)

30. Detail from *Wild Horses,* a woodcut by Hans Baldung Grien, 1534.

31. *The Horse Tamers* (detail). Rome, Piazza Quirinale. (Photo: Alinari.)

32. Detail from the Frontispiece.

33. *Silenus.* Engraving of an antique statue from F. de Clarac – *Musée de Sculpture,* Paris 1841.

34. *The Hunchbacked Beggar.* Bronze, 3rd century B.C. East Berlin, Staatliche Museen. (Photo: Museum.)

35. Detail from the Frontispiece.

36. *Death on a Pale Horse.* Etching by Joseph Haynes after J. H. Mortimer, 1784. London, British Museum. (Photo: Museum.)

37. *The Night Mare.* Caricature of C. J. Fox. By R. S., 1799. London, British Museum. (Photo: Museum.)

38. *The Night Mare.* Caricature of William Pitt. Attributed to Temple Webb, 1795. London, British Museum. (Photo: Museum.)

39. *John Bull's Night Mare.* By R. Seymour, 1828. London, British Museum. (Photo: Museum.)

40. *Napoleon Dreaming in his Cell at the Military College.* By G. Cruikshank, 1814. London, British Museum. (Photo: Museum.)

41. *Louis the Fat Troubled with the Night Mare.* By G. Cruikshank, 1823. London, British Museum. (Photo: Museum.)

42. *The Nightmare or The Source of the Nile.* Anon. print, *c.* 1798.

43. *The Nightmare.* By J. H. Fuseli, 1810. Pencil and Wash. Zurich, Kunsthaus. (Photo: Museum.)

44. Detail of *Mars and Venus.* Engraving by H. Goltzius, 1585. Vienna, Albertina. (Photo: Museum.)

45. *Count Ugolino.* Engraving after lost painting by J. H. Fuseli, 1806. London, British Museum. (Photo: Museum.)

46. *Religious Fanaticism attended by Folly trampling upon Truth.* Mezzotint by J. H. Fuseli, *c.* 1780–90.

47. *The Dream of Eleanor.* By G. Kininger, *c.* 1795. Vienna, Albertina. (Photo: Museum.)

48. *A Nightmare.* By N. Abildgaard, *c.* 1800. Kunstmuseet I Sorø. (Photo: Museum.)

49. *The Sleep of Reason Produces Monsters.* Etching by Goya, 1796–8. Vienna, Albertina. (Photo: Museum.)

50. *Capricho no. 9.* Etching by Goya, 1796–8. Vienna, Albertina. (Photo: Museum.)

51. *Rêve.* Lithograph after Tony Johannot, *c.* 1830. Paris, Bibliothèque Nationale. (Photo: Museum.)

52. *Cauchemar.* Engraving after Tony Johannot, 1830. Oxford, F. Haskell collection.

53. *Smarra.* Lithograph after Tony Johannot, 1845. Paris, Bibliothèque Nationale. (Photo: Museum.)

54. *The Racing Nightmare* (detail). Lithograph after A. C. Havell, 1891.

55. *The Nightmare.* Engraving after J. H. Fuseli by W. Raddon, 1827. London, British Museum. (Photo: Museum.)

Index